AF207357

ISBN 978-0-9861014-0-3

Contents

Introduction

Welcome to Oh Crap Potty Training! This is the definitive guide to potty training. I'm Jamie and I will be your tour guide on this really cool journey. What? Cool journey? Yep, you heard right. The first step I want you to take in beginning potty training is to wrap your head around what a very cool milestone this is. Walking and talking, learning to read and tie shoes and ride bikes are all really cool milestones that we, as parents, **look forward** to. Potty training, however, fills us with dread, right? It shouldn't. One of the coolest things I've discovered about potty training is that it's your first glimpse into **how** your child learns. Every child learns — and therefore potty trains —a little differently, and you get great insight into your child's learning methods and curve.

This is version 3.0 of this book. If you don't know my history as a potty trainer, you can check my bio on the website (www. http://www.jamieglowacki.com). Despite a solid decade of experience potty training, my business exploded when we opened the consulting forum in the summer of 2011, and I began to work with lots of people all at the same time, which gave me insight into emerging new trends, new problems, and new parenting methods and styles. I also discovered that there really isn't ONE method for potty training, because even though there's a necessary component to all successful methods — to potty train, you must take the diapers off the child — children are different, and respond to different approaches. In this book, I'm going to teach you the most painless way to get your child out of diapers, but more important, I'm going to present the answers to any questions you might have going forward from that point. Bottom line: all kids react differently to not wearing a diaper and that, my friends, is what everyone fears. We'll get into all the nitty gritty details soon enough. First, though, I need to do some myth busting, and you need to do some mental prep. Then I'll walk you through the first few days of potty training, and finally, we'll get to all the potential questions you might have.

I used to call this a three day plan. There's a reason there are a million "three day potty training methods" out there on the internet. It takes roughly three days for the average child to get over the major hump of potty training. But your child is unique, as is your relationship with her. Every child has his own learning curve and — this is a big AND — you have an emotional investment in this. One of the reasons I can potty train someone else's child in a day is that I don't have an emotional investment. It's not MY child. You and your child have a wonderfully strong bond; this is both to your advantage and disadvantage. So, yes, some bumps can appear on this road. Over the years, I've found that some parents get all wrapped up in potty training in three days flat. This creates the very pressure you want to avoid when potty training. If you put pressure on the process, it will collapse.

I'll also throw this in; we all know how very different our children are from one another, and yet somehow the media has led us to think that there's a cookie cutter version of potty training that will work for every kid. Impossible. How could one way work identically on very different people? Kind of weird when you think of it that way, isn't it?

It will take most kids about 3-7 days for the potty training to 'click.' For some kids the process may be longer, while for others it will be shorter. We won't know what kind of kid you have until you jump in, but no matter how fast or slow the process is, it's all okay and expected. It's the same as learning to read. Some kids pick it up quickly and seemingly intuitively, while others take longer to string letters together into sounds (the latter is more common, btw). I'm going to give you markers to track **progress**, because that's what's important here. This whole thing is about progress, not perfection. What we are going to be doing is bringing your child's awareness from **Clueless** to **I Peed** to **I'm Peeing** to **I Have to go Pee**. That's it. Each segment can take roughly a day. Some kids cruise through one component and stall out on another. Again, we won't know until you jump in.

You should notice that nothing here is written in stone as an absolute. We are dealing with little human beings. Their brains aren't mature yet, but these little people are very capable of thinking their own thoughts, and they come chock full of their own personality. I'm passionate about potty training because of the many differences between one child and another, so having said that, you need to keep your child's individual personality in the front of your mind as you go through this process, yes?

On that note, what you are reading is a curriculum. I don't hold the magic keys. You do. I am a potty training expert, but you are the expert on your child. If I say something that doesn't resonate, ditch it. I do my best to back up everything I say with a healthy dose of WHY but I'm happy to be wrong.

A few quick side notes before we begin. Throughout this book, I've shared a lot of blog posts I've written. I highly suggest you subscribe to my blog. I learn new things every day from clients and I keep my thoughts very up to the minute there. Plus, I've been told I'm funny.

In using this book, I highly recommend you read up through Chapter 5: How to Ditch the Diapers. I've kept the how-to as simple as possible because some people cruise right through the process with nary a question. The rest of the book is all — and I mean **all** — I know about potty training. It's an overwhelming number of what-ifs and how to fix them. This sort of thing may be your idea of fun reading, but I don't recommend overwhelming yourself with potential problems that may never exist for you.

I will mention clients and specific situations throughout. For privacy, all names have been changed. I've also blended various scenarios for brevity.

I cuss, my humor has been termed "sick" and I'm pretty sarcastic. It's not out of disrespect. I make my living talking about poop; I have to have some levity. I don't mean to offend nor do I take such a major milestone lightly. Still, sometimes no word other than "f**k" will do.

I'm thrilled you've chosen me to help you on this journey. Now...are you ready to kick some potty training butt?

Chapter 1: In the Beginning...

First off, although I'll admit that I really like the word "crap," I tend to use "pee" and "poop" with my own child, and those are the words I'll use in this book. I think they are pretty commonplace and fit the bill nicely. However, don't feel you have to use them. You should decide on your own family's lingo. Any words will do, as long as there is consistency.

One thing I'll be talking about quite a lot is mixed messages. We send our children many mixed messages about potty training, and I think that's one of the reasons it's become such a huge ordeal. The words you use are just one example. I don't care if you choose to say poop, crap, she-she, urine, BM, peeps, caca, doody, lala, foofoo...whatever. Just be consistent. Bear in mind, this word will be said VERY LOUDLY in church, at the library, in the market. Be sure it's a word you are comfortable with at high volume and frequency. I've worked with parents who say "caca" at home and then try to get away with "BM" in public. The toddler mind doesn't work that way. Don't confuse the issue.

Regarding the phrase "potty training," I know some parents object to the term. I've heard it said that training is for animals, not children. Let's just agree that "training" is synonymous with "learning" for our purposes. After all, even as an adult, you "train" in something in order to learn it. As an analogy, when you get a new job, you receive training. Someone already skilled guides you through your new duties. On your first day of work, does your boss sit and wait for your cues that you're ready? Ready for what? When you make a mistake does your boss get distraught and fire you?

No. Most likely, you are clearly told what is expected of you and shown how to do it. When you make mistakes, your boss gently tells you what you did wrong and how do it right. After a certain amount of time, you're expected to have mastered your new duties. There you go — that's potty training.

I also like to compare potty training to learning to walk. I've always been amazed by kids learning to walk. Let's face it — they get around much faster by crawling. So why take on this new skill? Because it's in our nature as humans to walk upright. It's also in our nature to pee and poop in designated areas. Even cultures that don't have plumbing have definitive places for excrement.

Think back to when your child learned to walk. You probably watched her constantly to make sure she didn't whack her head on something. You put her between your legs and held her hands and helped her along. You cheered her on and smothered her with kisses. You showed off her new skill to anyone who set foot in your house. When she fell and cried, you picked her up, dusted her off and encouraged her to try again. Did you give her stickers or M&Ms for learning · to walk? Did you beg and plead and ask her a million times a day if she felt like walking? Did you get all freaked out? Did you consult everyone you knew and research the topic endlessly? Probably not. You knew your child should start walking around 12 months give or take a couple of months on either side. You might have bought a little push toy to help the process. You **would** have been concerned if she was 18 months old and not showing any sign of walking. Generally speaking, you probably used your parental intuition and your knowledge of your child to help her learn how to walk.

Ideally, you'll have a similar philosophy toward potty training.

One thing I've always found bizarre is that parents assume that potty training is just something the child is going to pick up. Why would they? They **might** realize it's in their future, but so is driving. The need to pee and poop is a primal one; learning to put it somewhere specific is social, and social behavior must be taught.

I like to remind parents that kids don't know the beauty of potty training. **The only thing they know is the comfort and safety of wearing a diaper.** This is completely uncharted territory. Since coming out of the womb, all they've known is a snug diaper. Seriously, some babies have a diaper on before their first nursing! It's like the ultimate security blanket. This is especially important to remember if you're met with resistance. Not wearing a diaper can feel strange, uncomfortable and unsafe to a small child. It's your job to guide your child through this new territory. After all, using the potty is a skill you've already mastered. Well, let's hope so anyway.

So let's get down to the nitty gritty. The number one question I'm most asked is "What's the trick?" Are you ready for the trick? The Big Trick of Potty Training? Memorize this. Study it intently. Are you sure you're ready?

YOU.

Let me repeat that. You, you, you, you, you, you.

YOU are the parent. YOU provide safety and boundaries for your child. YOU are the teacher. YOU provide a loving environment where it's safe to grow. Again, YOU provide the boundaries. It is your job to nurture your child to their fullest potential. It's your job to instill dignity and self-respect.

More than just you, it's your COMMITMENT. This is a big deal, your commitment. Potty training is not rocket science by any means. I can tell you what to do until I'm blue in the face, but until you decide you are committed to the process, it's not going to fly with your child.

When I say commitment, I mean your commitment to consistency. This is a new skill you are teaching your child. Humans learn by repetition. I repeat; humans learn by repetition.

Even as an adult, have you learned a skill, then not used it consistently and lost it? Of course you have. Pick a skill. I've tried to learn knitting for years. I start and then I don't do it enough and I forget. I have to learn all over again every time. It's ever so slightly easier the next time, but not by much. How about playing a musical instrument? Consistent practice is vital. Very few people make significant progress by just playing once in a while. Think of your job. Skills that are now second nature once took a lot of thought and concentration. After enough repetition,things just sink in.

While potty training, you need to be consistent and firm. By firm, I mean 'without question', not aggressive or pushy. I would say "firm" can be a pretty contentious word in parenting these days. I have so many clients who are afraid of being firm. Being firm and meaning business is **good**, and it doesn't have to look mean. Many modern parents are afraid of being an authoritative presence in their home. Most of the time this is because their parents were over-the-top authoritative (authoritarian) and it left a sour taste in their mouth and/or resulted in years of therapy. Still, there's a happy medium. Your child needs you to be the authority figure, and wants you to be in charge. To have no boundaries is like a free fall through life. So don't be afraid of being assertive and firm. Again, not mean, not aggressive or pushy. We'll definitely touch on this throughout the book for clarity.

Consistency is how your child learns effortlessly. How many times did you sing the ABC song before your child sang it through by herself? Did you sing it a couple of times every couple of weeks and then expect her to sing it for grandma? I don't know about you but I think I sang that song 20 times an hour, over and over and over. Remember, too, that **children love consistency**. All children, even adventurous children, love routine. Read it again. Sing it again. Build it again. Things we repeat feel safe to our kids. They know what to expect and are prepared. Spirited children, especially, need and crave routine.

It's amazing to me that we would expect a child to step up to the task of potty training without this consistency. Examples of inconsistency are to occasionally have them go on the pot, but sometimes put on a diaper, or to sometimes demand they go on the pot, and other times let it slide. This results in such a constant giving and taking away of responsibility that it's no wonder so many power struggles ensue. Doesn't that make sense? It does to me and yet I often hear these statements:

"We don't really care right now."

"We're going to wait till she's ready."

"We're just being really casual about it."

I'll address the latter two statements in just a moment. For now, let's look at, "We don't really care right now". What I think people mean when they say this is that they're not really committed — that it's not a high priority in their lives right now. Which is fine. Just be honest with yourself. If it's not a high priority with you it's not going to be a high priority for your child either. I spend a great deal of time in my classes on this topic. Often, parents realize that they are afraid to commit because they don't know what to do and they're concerned that they might fail.

More often, though, parents feel something along the lines of, "Eh...we just don't feel like it's that important right now," "We are doing other things," or "What's the rush? She'll do it. I mean, she's not going to college in diapers, right?" True, your child is most likely not going to college in diapers. But I routinely get clients who've had to delay preschool because of a lack of potty training. Last September, two sets of parents came to me after their children were asked to leave kindergarten for not being trained properly. So yeah, it might not be vital right this minute, but it's going to creep up on you faster than you know. And I'll be beating this particular horse till it's good and dead — the longer you wait to potty train, the harder it gets.

Another reason behind the "we don't care" attitude is that something is happening in your life and you know you can't give potty training the attention it needs. That's completely understandable **if** there's actually going to be a break in the action at some point. I remember a mom emailing me. She and her husband were both medical residents and she was expecting her second child. She felt life was too hectic to potty train. To this, I responded, "It's not going to be any less hectic for your family for a good long time." True, if you are moving or traveling, now might not be the best time to potty train. But if your life itself is busy, you are going to have to carve out some time regardless.

I won't lie to you. This process is going to require attention and focus on your part. Potty training is all you will be thinking about for at least a week or so. However, it will be — it should be — effortless on your child's part.

Do I think it should be a high priority no matter what's happening in your life right now? Yes, absolutely. Here's why:

1. **Environment.** One year of one child using disposable diapers uses two full grown trees. Do the math and it's downright scary. There's just no reason to prolong diaper use. Even if you use solely cloth — which very few people do — you're still using valuable resources such as water for cotton processing and diaper-washing.

2. **Landfill space.** It's estimated that disposable diapers take anywhere from 250-500 years to decompose. They are accumulating in our landfills at an alarming rate. What's worse is very few people dispose of the poop in the toilet before throwing away the diaper — did you even know you're supposed to do that? — so there's the added problem of raw sewage in our landfills.

3. **Your child's dignity.** This is one I'll repeat over and over. We both know just how smart your child is. Doesn't he deserve the dignity of not crapping in a diaper and still worse, sitting in it? Really think about that. Think about where your child is developmentally and just how undignified this is. I hear parents talk about giving their child self-esteem. Self-esteem comes from mastering a task, from gaining dignity and self-respect. Potty training is a way you can give this to your child.

"We're just going to wait till she's ready"

Oh. Boy. As reasons for delaying potty training go, this is the big one. I'd say this particular rationale is responsible for more potty training drama than any other. If you really follow this thought through, it doesn't make any sense. First, I'd like to point out some realities of toddlerhood. In what other area of development do wait until your child is ready? Do you wait until he's ready to go to bed? (I sincerely hope not. That's another book entirely). How about when your toddler decides she's ready to play with knives? If you have errands to run, do you stay home until your toddler is ready to leave the house? What about if she's not ready to get in her car seat? Do you drive off anyway?

I'm being a bit facetious, of course, but I'm just trying to point out that there are non-negotiables with our children. We don't let toddlers decide too much on their own; their brains just aren't fully formed yet. We are constantly deciding things for them, for their well-being, developmental and emotional growth, and safety. These non-negotiables exist simply because we, as the more experienced humans, understand some things better than our toddlers do.

One of my favorite books in the parenting world is *Simplicity Parenting* by Kim John Payne. The most fabulous concept I got from his book is that we are, in general, offering our children too many choices. Further, we are expecting them to have the thought processes of an adult. Children don't have fully developed frontal lobes, which are responsible for judgement. We cannot present them with unlimited choices. If we do, they will not make good long-term choices. To expect them to do so is to rush childhood, which is wild when you think about it. I feel that the idea of "waiting till they are ready" falls into the category of giving the toddler more choices than he can reasonably handle.

In my experience, "waiting till they are ready" leads to disasters. You've probably heard, unless you live in a cave, that "ready" is around 3 years. Not so. That's past ready. Once a child is 3, he is well into the process of individualization, which is the process by which he begins to realize he is his own person and has his own free will and can make his own choices. Hmmm. What do you suppose will happen if he decides he doesn't want to use the potty, and that the diaper is working just fine for him?

I'll tell you what will happen: you'll have a drama-filled disaster. It's really hard to potty train children over 3. They have free will and they know how to use it.

So this notion of "waiting till they're ready" is somewhat ludicrous. You are going to have to give potty training some attention and focus, whether you tackle it when your child is 2, 3, 4, 5 or 6 years old. Regardless of the child's age, she is still going to need your attention, help, and guidance. Please don't wait until she is beyond 4 — talk about giving her low self-esteem. If you wait that long, you should probably save for therapy, not college.

There's also the question of what, exactly, "ready" means. If you are waiting for a magical day when your child up and decides diapers are no longer for him and just does his business on the toilet, keep dreaming. This child is a fictional character. Okay, not completely fictional, but this child is **extremely** rare. And no matter what you've heard about other parents' kids, I have to be honest - I think some moms who say their kid just decided on his own one day have sort of fudged the details. I know this is shocking, but some moms are competitive. Also, I think potty training pains are like labor pains, and the details get fuzzy over time.

I'd say my biggest fight as a potty trainer is this "wait till they are ready" business. The only reason I do fight is for the kids; in my job, I have the dubious luxury of seeing big numbers, and I see where this can lead. Frankly, it can lead to full-blown disasters. It can lead to 6-year-olds requesting diapers so they can poop. A friend of mine told me about a parenting forum where a mom was talking about her 6-year-old wearing pull-ups to his first sleepover. He was mortified when he got home. He told his mom, "This is your fault." There you have it. Despite all this, the other moms on the forum were saying things like, "Don't worry. He'll do it when he's ready." OMG. So maybe some kids **will** be going to college in diapers.

The whole point is this: some kids will never be "ready" on their own. Also, trying to potty train an older child is hard. I also suspect that the muscles used to control holding and releasing pee and poop are developing around 2 years of age. If you wait beyond 3 years of age to potty train, it's as though these muscles have learned to **not** be able to hold the pee. This is my own theory based upon what I know about muscle development, combined with the large number of incontinence issues I've seen in kids over 3.

Dr. Brazelton is a very famous pediatrician who has become the foremost advocate of late potty training. He's promoted late potty training and the whole "wait till they're ready theory" for around the last 7 years, and pretty aggressively at that. It also turns out that he is a paid spokesperson for Pampers. Pretty clear conflict of interest, don't you think? Bear in mind that disposable diapers are a $450 **billion** dollar a year business, so there's a pretty high stake in keeping you mucked up about potty training. If you'd like to read my very hardcore view (meaning, I drop the f-bomb every two sentences) you can check out my blog post "I'm Pissed and I'm Naming Names".

Rather than thinking about readiness, I'd like you to think in terms of capability, as in, "Is my child capable of learning this right now?"

In expressing this idea to parents, I often use the example of my son learning to tie his shoes. He never really asked me if he could learn this skill, and Velcro had certainly made my life easier. Still, I know that learning to tie shoes generally happens sometime around kindergarten, and I think it's a pretty important life skill. I therefore made a concerted effort, once he hit that age, to buy only shoes with laces. I knew if I bought Velcro, I'd cave in to the morning rush. Life will always happen, so if we want to change something, we have to make an effort. I set aside 30 minutes every morning to teach my son to tie his shoes. There was a fair amount of frustration; the worst was on my part for feeling inept, or that I was not being a good teacher, despite the fact that I've been tying shoes for years. The whole process required a fair amount of patience from us both. Still, after 6 days of consistently attending to this task, voila! My son can tie his own shoes. Did he show signs of readiness? No, not really. Rather, I used an outside age marker and my "Spidey Mom Sense" to determine that he was **capable**.

In my experience, many not-yet-potty trained kids are capable, and may even show outward signs of readiness. But I think in our very busy lives, these subtle signs go undetected. I also think most people think the desire and willingness to sit and go potty on the toilet will increase with time. As in, if he asks to go on the potty once in a while right now, next month he will be asking to go everyday. Again, this is just my experience, but I've found that if you don't seize the appropriate window, the kid just moves on and forgets about it. In other words, the interest in using the toilet does not increase exponentially with time — it peaks and goes away.

Most moms, probably including you, are reading this book because you know deep in your heart that your child is ready. Go with that feeling. I'm going to help you tap into your own intuition about potty training. I'm a big believer in "go with your gut".

"We're just being really casual about it."

I hear this one a lot, and to some extent, it's fine. Just know that if you're really casual about potty training, your child will also be really casual about it. I should clarify that by casual, I don't mean you have a casual demeanor. I mean you have your child pee in the potty once or twice a day, or you sometimes put a diaper on him, and sometimes don't. The problem with this approach is there comes a time when it's no longer appropriate. Maybe your chosen preschool or kindergarten won't allow your child attend untrained. Or you were fine with the casual approach for a 2- or 3-year old, but now your child is 4 and you feel like it's time to get serious. Stay casual too long, and you will have missed the window of opportunity; consequently, it becomes infinitely harder to train the child. You'll be facing nothing but power struggles, and your life will turn into a living hell.

I also think "being casual about it" sends a very mixed message. Let's look at this through toddler eyes. Remember toddlers are sponges; they learn very quickly. Also remember that toddlers are linear thinkers with no concept of time. Let's say you start with casual potty training. You announce that you are potty training, but what you mean is that you are going to have your child pee when it's convenient, such as in the morning before getting dressed. Or in the evening before bath. Your child is going to literally learn this: potty training means peeing on the potty *sometimes*, but not all the time.

Let's say you take this approach for about a year, which is what usually happens. Then the time comes when the potty training needs to be **done** already. You say, "Okay, now it's *really* time to potty train."

Your child is going to do a toddler version of "WTF? I've got this down. I'm doing what she asked." In switching approaches, you've just added a complicated additional step to the whole process. As a result, you have to re-teach the concept of what potty training means. Do you see?

I think a lot of parents expect that the child will naturally realize that one day, he's going to go pee and poop on the toilet, but in reality, that's a big conceptual leap to expect from a toddler. Why would your child make that assumption when all he's known since birth is a diaper?

The whole casual approach makes me cringe. I'd say a good 80% of my current clients are parents who took this approach and now have an older child in diapers. Then they have to call me in. It is not easy to potty train 4- and 5-year-olds — trust me. I'm not judging at all, but **IT'S JUST SO MUCH EASIER WHEN YOU POTTY TRAIN AT THE**

APPROPRIATE TIME! Heavy on the capitals, I know, but I feel that strongly about this.

Most children between 18 and 24 months begin to show an interest in the toilet. Often this has more to do with the toilet itself, the bathroom, and the spinning toilet paper than it does with a bodily function. It's also an interest in mimicking mom and dad. This interest doesn't necessarily signal any readiness to potty train; I always look for other markers. This brings us the next big issue in potty training.

Chapter 2: When to Start

Let me state this simply: *when is almost more important than how.* Unequivocally, potty training is easiest when done between the ages of 20 and 30 months. It certainly can be done earlier or later, with caveats. For instance, most children younger than 20 months won't connect the dots as fast as older kids, which means you'll need to be more responsible for acting on their cues (as opposed to expecting them to act on their own) than you would be if they were older.

However, before 20 months is unbelievably easier than after 30 months. Kids over 30 months are that much more sophisticated and skilled at manipulation. They know the power of choice and free will. My mom likes to say, "You want to do it before they know they have a choice in the matter." Anyone with a 3-year-old can tell you they are very adept at exerting their will. Your power struggles will be huge. And guess what? You won't win.

Smack-dab in the middle of that 20-30 month age range is best for most people. Right around 24 months is ideal. At this age, your child is eager to please, is connecting a lot of the dots in the big world around him, is still malleable, and is dying for more responsibility. Think about it. Kids at this age love helping and feeling important. They want to help cook and clean and do chores around the house — it's the perfect time to hand them their very own responsibility. You want to take advantage of this eager-to-please phase. It's natural and it's good and, unfortunately, it will go away. Trust me.

Mind you, there are always going to be exceptions. More recently, I've seen an increase in moms who know their kids are very capable of potty training before 20 months. And of course, there are plenty of children who potty train just fine in the 30-36 month age range. Still, in my experience, the 30-36 month age range is when things start getting tricky. And in case you didn't get my memo, waiting until after 3 is going to bring you struggles. We'll deal with the specific issues associated with younger and older kids in the later chapters.

Why this time frame?

1. There are certain "windows of opportunity" in development, during which a developmental task can be accomplished with the least amount of conscious effort on the part of the child. There are many such windows of opportunity during childhood. For example, weaning. Many kids wean at 12 months, because it's usually very easy to do at that particular age. Four months, 12 months, 24 months and 30 months are documented windows of opportunity for easy weaning. Can it be done at other times? Sure, it just requires a little more effort on the part of both mother and child. Similarly, there's a window of opportunity for learning a language. Researchers and parents alike know how effortlessly a child picks up a second language before the age of 5. The same is true for learning a first language. I once worked with a child who had been secluded in a studio apartment for all of her 5 years of life with her drug-addicted mother. Because of her limited social exposure, she missed the window of opportunity to learn her first language, English. To this day, she requires major

speech therapy, and struggles in school. If you want to potty train with the least amount of effort, the window of opportunity is between 20 and 30 months. It's just easier, that's all.

This period of time is also a developmental window during which there appears to be almost a lull in learning new skills. You child has probably learned the basics, like eating, walking, and working through separation anxiety. During this period, he is really just honing his skills. Nothing too momentous is being "worked out" developmentally during this time. Note that windows are relative to one another, though, so if your child has had delays in other big milestones, he will naturally be a bit delayed in potty training.

2. Teaching a child to use the potty imparts her with dignity and self-respect. At this age, your child is learning at the speed of light. You're probably amazed and amused by what she is now capable of. CAPABLE OF. Do not underestimate what your child is capable of. I see tons of parents gleefully showing off their child's genius, while that same kid is sitting in her own poop. That's not right. It's insulting to your child's intelligence to think she can't learn this new skill.

3. For several reasons, if you wait too long after 30 months, the process of potty training becomes a chore for you as well as for your child. There will be fights and power struggles, and things will get ugly fast. It will take soooo much longer. In my experience, if your child isn't fully trained by 4, the likelihood of a child being a bed wetter

are increased by 50%. You want to try on low self-esteem? Try going to your first sleepover and wetting the bed.

4. Also, as I've mentioned, after 30 months your child will be well into the process of individualization, that psychological process in which your child learns that he is his own person, and that he is separate and distinct from you. This process is marked by defiance and resistance as he learns to express his free will. This process is normal, but things get ugly if you wait until then to potty train. There will be a power struggle and for the first time ever, you child will literally be holding all the power, in the form of pee and poop. You will not win.

5. This ideal potty training time frame is usually accompanied by other markers, which I look for even before I look at age:

- Does your child retreat to a corner or private place to poop?
- Can your child recite the "ABC song"?
- Can your child COMMUNICATE his needs? By this I mean:
  - Can your child somehow ask for water, juice or milk when he's thirsty?
  - Can your child somehow ask for a snack when he's hungry?
  - Can your child throw a tantrum for candy at the market?
  - Can your child throw a tantrum for just about *anything*?

If your child is retreating to some private place — any place: under the table, another room, maybe even just turning his back — to poop, it is ABSOLUTELY time to start potty training. This means your child is equating pooping with privacy, which is a natural and correct progression. Your child is showing embarrassment. To be clear, these bodily functions are normal and you should not embarrass your child about them. However, with socialization comes a sense of shame in performing bodily functions in front of others. If you were sitting in my class and pooped in your pants, you'd be embarrassed. I'm warning you - if you don't recognize this sign of readiness and act on it, your child will soon forget to be embarrassed. When this happens, you end up with a 5-year-old who's not bothered at all by pooping in his pants.

In my experience, the "ABC song" is a rough — but by no means definitive — gauge of where your child is developmentally. Kids who can recite the song have learned some language and, most likely, they've learned it through repetition. So maybe your kid isn't busting out with full paragraphs of speech. If he can say his ABCs, he's probably ready. Again, I'm just going by my own experience; I've just seen a correlation between the ability to recite this song and ease of potty training.

Tantrums are due to your child WANTING something — anything — and you not giving it. If your child is aware of thirst, hunger, and desires (wants), and can act on those awarenesses, then your child is perfectly capable of regulating her bodily functions; your child is ready to be potty trained.

Just in case I've haven't beaten you over the head enough with this time frame I'll reiterate. Between 20 and 30 months is the perfect time to potty train. Trust me. It's almost freaky how much resistance you will encounter if you attempt to potty train after 30 months.

Now, let's say your child has all of the markers I've been talking about, and you're just not convinced of his readiness. Or you are wildly unsure. Or you don't want to eff this up. Or everyone, but everyone is telling you that 24 months is too early to potty train.

I CAN NOT STRESS THIS ENOUGH: if you are attempting to potty train and you have major doubts, it will NOT go well for you. I have seen it time and time and time again. YOU MUST BELIEVE YOU ARE DOING THE RIGHT THING. You must know that your child is capable of this. It's okay to be a little unsure but you must be determined. If you are in two camps — sure and unsure — your child will be too. It will look like a hot mess. I have no other words to explain this phenomenon by which your kid picks up on your attitude other than woo-woo words, like 'vibe' and 'energy.' If your mind isn't made up, your child will pick up on it and mirror being sure and unsure. Whenever I get a client whose situation suggests a lack of determination, I usually start with the "Are you sure you are committed?" speech. My blog is peppered with the importance of determination and we'll discuss it more in later chapters. I used the word 'vibe' earlier because I'm all airy fairy, but if you're not, "non-verbal cues" works too. Here's just one blog post:

As many of you know, I used to not be a dog person. Since we got a dog, I'm a TOTAL dog person. And since I have a dog and 5-year-old, I can't help but notice many similarities between these two small beings. It didn't take me long to figure out how much information our dog receives from NON-VERBAL CUES. This dog (and while I love her, I don't think she's special in this respect) knows the different sounds my pots and pans make and which one is most likely to yield a snack. She knows that when my coffee starts brewing, it's time to wake up and pee. But mostly she senses excitement, anticipation and fear in ME. And she reacts accordingly.

A few weeks back, we were going on a road trip to see my best friend. Stella (the dog) was coming with us, but she didn't seem to get that. That morning, the packing, the anticipation, the energy of going on a trip was driving her BANANAS. She was under foot and whining. I finally put her in the car to wait for us and she settled right down. SHE KNEW SOMETHING WAS HAPPENING AND SHE WASN'T SURE WHAT. Once in the car, she was okay. Like, "I'm going with them. Okay. Cool."

OUR CHILDREN ARE NO DIFFERENT. They are just figuring out the big world around them. They are sensitive and on high alert for new information, largely from non-verbal cues. They are watching, listening and, more importantly, SENSING what it is we are feeling. And they are going to react accordingly.

I think most people don't even realize how sensitive our children are because we TALK to them and assume they understand. So even if we are shaking with fear, we assume that we can talk our way out of it. But with little kids, that's not true. They pick up that vibe way more than the words.

I've seen the mere mention of potty training drain the color from a parent's face, send waves of panic through her body and set off the craziest thread of comments on Facebook. So many parents jump into the first day of potty training with that very same vibe: one of panic, dread and fear. And then they can't figure out why their child is resisting or kicking up dirt. Why on earth would a child want to do something that's got Mom so wound up?

Imagine going to your child's first dental visit with that panic and dread. Yikes. Good luck with that.

So how do you fix it? How do you stay calm and trust your gut?

You think of this as a developmental milestone — which it is — not a potential war. You know in your heart when your child is capable of doing this. You don't post on Facebook when you are ready to start and get 64 varying opinions. You realize your child is an individual and will have his own learning curve. You recognize that he may not do this just like your best friend's kids. And you realize this is not a measurement of your parenting. It's just something you are teaching your child.

Panic, fear and dread will only put more difficulties in your path.

Relax. And breathe...

Since the original writing of this book, more and more parents are choosing to begin potty training between 18 and 22 months. This was actually the expected time to potty train a generation ago. Modern moms training during this period are having huge success, because the potty just becomes another thing the child is learning; it's not wrapped up in any other drama, like the drama of being 2. I will specifically address kids under 20 months and over 30 months in the chapter of that title.

For now, let's bust up some myths and misconceptions that might be blocking your path to easy potty training.

Chapter 3: Myths and Misconceptions

Okay, so we're clear on when to potty train. Now I'd like to talk about some common myths and misconceptions — some widely held beliefs you may have heard of or read. Some are so common, they've almost become law. They've infiltrated daycares, playgrounds and community centers. Some are convenient soundbites that I often read or hear about. I'm going to deconstruct them here, so we can get logical about all of this.

Warning: You may need to use some common sense here, so be prepared.

Take a moment to think about whether these statements are true or false:

1. It's best to wait until your child gives you signals.
2. Boys are harder to train than girls.
3. It's easier to train for pee first, then tackle poop.
4. You should put the potty chair out before you start training so your child can get used to it.

Myth #1: It's best to wait until your child gives you signals.

False. We've sort of covered the idea of "waiting till they're ready," but let's give it some more thought. What does a parent mean by, "I'm going to wait till he gives me signals that he's ready"? What signals? Some not-yet-potty-trained kids start staying dry during naps, or wake up dry in the morning, but not usually. Some kids show an interest in the toilet, but others don't ever show an interest. Are you waiting for your child to wave a flag that says, "I have to pee"? Remember, all your child has known is a diaper. What signal could they possibly give when they don't know what is they are signalling? Just think about it. How do you signal for a brand new action? Once potty training has begun, sure, your child will have signals. For instance, she might do a pee-pee dance. This could be the classic hopping from foot to foot. Other "dances" or signals could include staying completely still. You might notice that she looks antsy or twitchy. Regardless of your individual child's signals that she has to pee, they develop once you've **begun** potty training, not before. To wait for a signal from your child that he is ready to begin potty training is inviting trouble.

Myth #2: Boys are harder to train than girls.

Really false. This one ticks me off. A lot. Mostly because so many people buy this crap. Close your eyes and give this some SERIOUS thought. Why on earth would this be true? Some people in my class have suggested it's because girls supposedly mature faster than boys. Perhaps this is true, but it becomes significant much later, like during the preteen years. Not so much at 2. When I see a group of 2-year-olds, they all seem on pretty even ground. It's all pretty much, "don't hit and please share." If anything, I think boys are EASIER to train than girls. They can pretty much pee anywhere. He's got to go in the parking lot? Just pull down the pants and pee on the tires. And this is just my own personal observation, but because a boy's equipment is outside and a girl's is neatly tucked away, I think boys do a much more prominent pee-pee dance. And mostly I refuse to believe that at this age, my son is not as smart as some girl! Use your common sense and intuition here. Boys are not harder to train than girls. There are some differences between the genders, but "different" doesn't mean "harder."

Myth #3: It's easier to train for pee first, then tackle poop.

This is absolutely false. I've heard this before but I don't even know how you'd approach training this way — put a diaper on for poop, or what? This is one of the oddest myths out there, but it IS out there, so I'm addressing it. Your child will very easily identify both pee and poop as bodily functions that need to go in the pot, even though the sensations accompanying them come from two different places. This is not to say that parents and children don't often have a difficult time with poop. Poop actually has its very own chapter. And I might point out that it's the longest chapter in the book. It's a big frigging deal that's recently gotten bigger.

For now, just remember your child has only known squishy poop against his butt. It sounds gross, but it's a sensation he knows and is comfortable with. And kids' little bodies generally produce an absurd amount of poop, usually quite effortlessly. The sensation of poop just sliding out and not hanging around is brand new and somewhat scary.

In general, we are a culture that disdains the very important bodily function of pooping, and that's what our kids learn. Given that, is it any wonder that some kids don't want to poop? Look at how you act about poop, both your own and your child's. You have to make this a very normal, important function for your child. From the time you are done reading this book until you begin potty training, you should be letting your child come with you to pee and poop. It's very important to have your child see that pooping is normal, it doesn't hurt, and its existence doesn't have to be veiled in secrecy. I highly suggest that if you or your partner is a *NY Times* kind of person, get things rolling by bringing your child with you. Have them sit on the floor and read, or you can read to them. Does that sound freaky to you? If it does, it's a good indicator that your poop values are a little more stringent than you thought. Loosen up...it will help your child.

All the time, I'll hear parents say something like, "Oh! We are total poop people. Very comfortable with it. Yup. No issues here." And then their kid has a hard time with poop. When I suggest they take their kid with them to poop, they freak out about how weird and gross that is. If this is weird and gross to you, that attitude will be conveyed to your child.

In any event, We'll hit it all in the poop chapter. Betcha' can't wait, huh?

Myth # 4 (and I saved the best for last!): You should put the potty chair out before you start training so your child can get used to it.

So false my head might blow off. I'm sure you've at least heard this, if you're not in fact already doing it. I applaud you for not sneaking up on your child and freaking them out, but please read on with a dash of common sense. The small potty chair was invented to be a less scary version of the big porcelain bowl. The toilet is indeed scary to a little kid. The size is scary, the flushing is overwhelming, and your child's butt is way too small for the seat. So some brilliant person invented a small pot that is just right!

Now I want to ask you a couple of questions. First, look around your house and play close attention to baby items: highchair, stroller, bouncy chair, and talking toys. I'm willing to bet that the small potty chair is the most innocuous piece of plastic in your house! Did you put the highchair out for your child to get used to it? No, you probably put it together and put her in it and took your first shower in weeks. Did you put your child in the highchair to "practice"? No, you probably put him in it to eat. And when he was done eating, you probably took him right out. Did you leave your stroller in the middle of the living room so she could get used to it? No, you strapped her in and went for a walk. Think about it!

Now another question. Would you let your child play around your toilet and bathroom to get used to it? Would you let your child throw things in the toilet? No, it's for one purpose only: pooping and peeing. We usually don't use containers for fecal matter for any other purpose.

Putting a potty chair out for your child to get used to it is useless and counter-productive. If you have already done this, you probably know that the chair has become a basketball net, a stroller, a hat, art supply storage, a matchbox car garage, a step stool and a doll pool. **Your child does not need to get used to the potty.** Putting it out ahead of actual potty training will only serve to lessen its magic. It's for one special purpose and that purpose only.

If you have been doing this, no worries. I'll tell you how to remedy the situation in Chapter 5.

When I start a class I like to ask everyone where they are in the potty training process. Most often I hear this: "Well, we put the potty chair out so he could get used to it. He sometimes sits on it. Sometimes he asks to go, but not with any regularity. Yesterday, he asked to sit on it in the morning but that was it. When he's naked, he usually sits on it, but when he's dressed he doesn't usually want to. So yeah, I guess he's kind of potty trained." Most of these parents report this as success. Sound at all familiar?

Kind of potty trained is like kind of pregnant. One pee on the pot in the morning is not potty trained. Using the pot while naked, at home, is not potty trained. I have to be honest here, and you may not like this: most of the parents I've worked with who put the pot out for their child to get used to it are really putting it out to see if she will up and decide to potty train herself. They harbor this secret fantasy that once the potty is out, their child will use it correctly. They haven't yet really committed to the process of potty training.

Once again, using the potty is a skill that must be learned, just like any other skill your child has learned. I'll repeat what I said in Chapter 1. Children learn by repetition. Therefore, if you put the pot out, you should be ready to consistently teach your child to use it.

I see all kinds of mixed messages and a lack of consistency in parents "trying" to potty train. A quick detour for a second to a blog post about "Trying":

Who doesn't love Yoda? I kinda fancy myself the Yoda of potty training. I know...whatever, Jamie. Still, one of my favorite connections between Yoda and potty training is this:

"Do or do not. There is no try." Direct quote from the wise green guy.

This goes right along with my theory of "kinda potty training." Or "trying" to potty train. You are either potty training or you are not. Trying does not enter the equation. If you are "trying," you are giving yourself an out. I often think about it in terms of smoking. A smoker trying to quit is still a smoker. They allow themselves to smoke in a moment of stress or when it gets too hard. A smoker who quits no longer smokes, regardless of the situation they might find themselves in.

Are you "trying" to potty train in order to give yourself an out? Why? Convenience? Or fear of failing? Not doing it right?

Have confidence in yourself and have faith in your kid. You both can do this, quickly, gently and effectively.

Do or do not. There is no trying.

Sounds an awful lot like, "Shit or get off the pot." Hmmm.

When you are "trying" to potty train, it often looks like this: you ask your child to pee on the potty, yet you turn around and put a diaper on him if it better suits the needs of your day. You ask your child to tell you when he has to pee but ask him to wait a minute while you finish whatever it is you're doing. You put the potty out so he can use it, but you don't teach him to use it consistently. Then the day comes, after months of "trying," when you've had it and get serious. Now you say, "I mean it." But your child has already learned that you don't.

So no, don't put the potty out for your child to get used to it. Put it out when you mean business. That is, you mean your child to put his business in it.

Common Misconceptions (or, Common Soundbites)

These are a couple of common misconceptions that I hear in neat little soundbites that warrant enough concern to discuss. They may or may not be on your worry list.

Soundbite #1: "But I don't want to push him."

This is probably the second-most-used soundbite in potty training, surpassed only by, "wait till he's ready." First, we need to examine where this phrase came from, and then we'll look at what it's become in modern parenting.

Not pushing a child to potty train, much like waiting for the child to be ready, started as a reaction to common potty training techniques in the 1940s, when children were strapped down to potty chairs at around 9 months of age. They were given soap suppositories to produce poop. They were often abused for accidents or left for hours to sit in their excrement. Just to be clear, **that is pushing a child**. And yes, it was horrible and abusive.

Then came Dr. Spock and a new wave of thought about child psychology, which introduced the notion that children are actually little humans with the capacity not only to feel pain, but to grow up with that pain into maladjusted big humans. The next 50 years gave slow birth to modern parenting philosophies, including the recent rise of attachment parenting (which isn't a new concept at all, actually). And so the pendulum began to swing. I believe that at present, we have swung about as far as possible from the parenting philosophies of the 40s.

Thanks to stupid, jerk *Time Magazine* and the infamous breast feeding cover (April, 2012) some modern parenting practices and philosophies have peaked in bitter controversy. Personally, I followed the tenets of the modern incarnation of attachment parenting, mostly during my son's first year. That is to say, I "wore" him in a baby carrier almost constantly, breastfed on demand, and co-slept. Then I stopped reading books and paying attention to "rules," and started to wing it based on what felt right. An excellent resource, which I'm not even sure uses the term "attachment parenting," is *The Continuum Concept* by Jean Liedloff. The major point I took away from this book is that children should be at the center of everyday life, so they know their place in the world. In this way, they learn that they are one of a whole, be it a family or a community, and they learn about the goings-on in daily life.

Through my work as a potty trainer, I see that things have gotten out of balance in many current parenting trends. In many cases, the child has **become** the center, rather than being **in** the center. The child gets all the focus and, often, gets a case of terminal specialness. What's also happened, as I talked about in Chapter 1, is that we have somehow come to think children can make their own decisions regarding what's best for them long term.

Now, you may find yourself bristling against me here, and that's okay. But I want to reiterate the point that every child needs to be nudged to learn new things. We are humans, and humans like to be good at what we attempt. Psychologists have found that blindly praising a child can actually limit them into doing only that at which they excel. We don't like to suck at things. As a result, humans — all humans, little or big — will stick to the status quo, simply because learning something means temporarily sucking at it.

We as parents are responsible for teaching our children and nudging them along in their learning. And check this out: if everything is hunky dory in your kid's life, what motivation does he have to change? Why would potty training be preferable to diaper-wearing? Think about that from the child's perspective. To him, there's no benefit. You are currently doing all the work. He doesn't need to think or stop what he's doing. You clean up the mess. The status quo is pretty darn good for him, so why change? The nudge to change comes from you, because — much like anything that requires learning and practice — we know he'll be better off for it on the other side.

I already gave you the example of my son learning to tie his shoes. Here's a post I wrote the week he started kindergarten:

 *From the Blog*

As many of you know, my son started kindergarten this week. That first day, I swear, I could hear my heart crack. Though I kissed him goodbye with a smile on my face and cheerfully said, "Have a great day!" I cried all the way home. It just seemed impossible that he's this big. I was also eating myself alive with anxiety.

I'm not sure if it's this way everywhere but at my son's school, you say goodbye at the schoolyard. This is big kid school. There was an orientation the week before. On the day of, you — the parent — don't go in. You don't help him find things or get him situated, and you don't have the opportunity to tell the teacher all of his idiosyncratic behavior.

I don't consider myself a helicopter mom — but then again, who does? Least of all, the helicopter moms! — but shit...what if a kid is bugging him and he doesn't know to ask for help? How does he know what to do and where to go? What if he gets lost in the shuffle? Does the teacher know that if he doesn't answer right away, he's thinking about it, not ignoring her? There are a billion things that only I know about this kid. How is this stranger going to know them????

Yeah. I was doing a big inner freak out. Huge.

And you know what? He was fine. As all my Facebook friends had reassured me he would be, he was fine. Better than fine. He loved it. He came home telling me things he thought he was the first to discover: "Mom! They have this thing called HOT LUNCH! You can BUY lunch at school." And he came home with a "big kid" attitude like I was completely stupid for suggesting things: "Moooom... kindergartners carry their OWN backpacks." Duh. Jeez.

He also has been falling asleep at 6:30, completely exhausted, even though they only have 15 minutes of recess (Do. Not. Get. Me. Started.)

And here's what I've learned this week, as it relates to potty training:

Kindergarten and potty training are both humongous milestones.

I was so sure that he was not ready. Someone, seemingly arbitrarily, choose this age to fling my kid to the wolves. Five. Ready. Like it or lump it. With a huge gulp, I did it, 'cause I really didn't have a choice. AND HE WAS TOTALLY READY. He likes the wolves. He does well with the wolves. OUR KIDS ARE READY EVEN WHEN WE ARE NOT.

This week has brought him more AUTONOMY than I could have tried to cultivate in a year. Today, I sent my kid with real money to make a real purchase, of his choice, on his own (a dollar for ice cream but still!!!) He wants to do his homework on his own because that's what big kids do. The first day, I picked him up in my arms and he said, "Put me down." He wants to be in the world as his own person. Bittersweet? Hell, yeah. But it's GOOD FOR HIM. For me to suppress this for my own emotional needs would be therapy-inducing and wrong.

LEARNING IS EXHAUSTING. Pascal's pre-school was very hip and urban. Located downtown, they would utilize the entire city as their playground.

*They walked up to 5 miles a day. For real. I was
sweating the 15 minute recess big time (Do. Not. Get.
Me. Started.) Yes, all kids need more of a physical
outlet than they tend to be allowed in school, but I
thought that he, especially, would miss it. Regardless,
he still comes home exhausted. Mental work is just
as tiring as physical work, maybe more so. Also,
TEACHING IS EXHAUSTING. His teachers look like
a truck ran over them by the end of the day. The bit
of homework he gets, exhausts me.*

*I'm blown away by the parallels between these two
milestones. And here's the thing: I didn't really have
much of a choice. Yeah, of course, there's always
a choice, but you know what I mean. Five is when
you start school. With fear and anxiety, I did what I
needed to do with a smile on my face. I'm asking you
to do the same thing with potty training.*

*Please potty train your child in the appropriate
time frame. You'll come out the other side with tiny
miracles. He'll be fine. She'll be fine. And yes, Mama,
you will be fine.*

Regardless of your parenting philosophy, I understand not
wanting to push your child. However, nudging things along
is NOT pushing. Pushing doesn't have to be abusive. Pushing
can be you, the parent, following through when your child
might not want to. Piano practice and homework are two big
things we, as parents, have to push. And you don't have to

be all tiger-mom about it; we're looking for the pendulum to stop somewhere in the middle.

I also remember teaching my son to ski. I had to do a lot of nudging past my son's fear that day, because I knew he was capable and I wasn't packing it in to get off the mountain and go home. I didn't "force" him, but I nudged him. A LOT.

I came to the conclusion (in a blog post, natch):

> *"[Teaching him to ski] made me [realize that] helping your child overcome these doubts and fears is part of parenting. I could have left the mountain, of course. But he LEARNED something that day, something that made him SHINE. Isn't learning something new often filled with fear and doubt?*
>
> *And there's always something amazing on the other side of that. Always."*

There's pride in learning something new, in overcoming something we thought we couldn't.

So, yes. Potty training will be your complete focus for the first week or so. But it will be so worth it when you see the look of pride on your child's face, that he did something he didn't know how to do last week. Yes, there can be some resistance. That first week of kindergarten, about ten kids kicked up so much resistance that you would have sworn torture was on the curriculum. I mean, they were screaming and kicking. Still, their parents, for various reasons, had to have them in school. And you know what? As soon as it became clear that there really wasn't another option, the kids settled down and now LOVE kindergarten. Once it became the new routine, it was just that: routine. But can you imagine if the parents hadn't "pushed" the issue?

We're going to hit resistance a bit later in the book, for sure. But for now, I don't want you to think any part of potty training is pushing your child to do something he's not capable of doing. No one goes into potty training thinking, "I'm gonna push this to the max. This kid is going to potty train whether she likes it or not," right? I mean, no one does that. Well, not anyone who's bought this book anyway. Those kind of parents don't usually make up my clientele.

However, I do see this happen all the time:

"Johnny, do you have to go? Do you have to pee now? Come on, let's go pee. Please? Mommy's going. Do you want to come with me? Come on, Johnny, I'm serious now. Story time is soon and we have to pee before we leave. I know you have to pee, you haven't peed all morning. Come ON. I want you to pee right now. Look, you're doing a little dance. Come on buddy, let's go pee. Please? DoyouhavetogoDoyouhavetogoDoyouhavetogo??????"

Nooooo...that's not aggressive at all.

This is from the very parents who don't want to "push" their children. I don't know about you, but it sounds awfully pushy to me. Most people don't even realize how much pressure they are putting on their child just by bugging him to death. A big part of potty training, as I teach it, is giving your child responsibility and following through with trust.

Soundbite #2: "Once your child is potty trained, accidents won't happen."

I love this one. I see it all the time in Facebook comments. I see it in blog posts. I hear it on the playground, usually accompanied by some sort of snide attitude: "A potty trained kid shouldn't have accidents."

When has your child ever learned something and then never made a mistake afterward? Ridiculous, no? To think that your child would never have an accident is weird. I wish there were a magic "potty training switch," and once you turned it on, it would be on forever. Yeah. Right.

Now, I know that from a logical perspective, we all realize this is false. Of course accidents happen. Still, I find that in reality, parents don't really expect them. Most don't prepare for it, and I'd say 90% of the parents I see expect FULL potty training in one or two days. You may have an all-star these first few days, but I assure you, accidents can still happen.

Potty training is a process. Your child will get better and better at it. This book will get you well on your way. Each week will get easier and easier, and you'll focus less and less on it. Accidents will happen, most often because we — the parents — forget (or ignore) pee-pee dances, or don't prompt the child. It's important to remember that accidents are just that; they're not intended. I like to tell parents to be prepared. Look, you're carrying around a diaper bag right now anyway. What's one more month of carrying around a change of clothes, just in case?

I like to say that accidents within the first week aren't accidents, but rather are learning tools. Both you and your child are still figuring this whole thing out. Of course, something's off if your child is ONLY ever having accidents, and is not making it to the potty at all. We'll discuss this later.

True 'accidents' are actually more likely to happen a few months into the process. This is when knowing how to use the potty has become nothing special. You no longer give verbal praise. You know your child knows his own signals, and you assume he'll tell you if he needs to go. That aside, big regressions warrant big scrutiny. Since I brought it up, let's discuss that a little further.

Regression

This problem often arises when parents are expecting another child and fear that initiating potty training with their toddler will end badly, with the child regressing as a newcomer enters the home. Simply defined, regression is moving backwards. Children sometimes do regress when a new sibling comes along. Most often, this is in the form of accidents. Personally, I have never seen a child regress all the way back to pre-potty trained. Any major transition — a new sibling, a move, a divorce — can trigger regression. The regression is your child's way of "acting out" his feelings because he's too young to articulate them in words. Acting out is always for attention. It saddens me when I hear people say, "Oh, she's just doing that for attention." Well, then pay attention. I'm talking a little more serious than your child being a total crackpot for Grandma.

While regression can be an issue, you should not delay potty training simply because you fear the possibility of a problem. First of all, you may not have one. Second, with all the work you're going to have with, say, the new baby, you want to have at least laid the potty training groundwork beforehand. Even if your toddler does regress, it is a thousand times easier to get back on track than to start from the beginning.

Also, don't assume your toddler will regress in the form of accidents. Some kids react to a major change in other ways. In the case of a new sibling, they might act out by hitting the new baby, biting you, or ignoring the newcomer entirely. Some kids will have no reaction whatsoever. We'll discuss more specifics in the *Random Thoughts* chapter.

Those are the biggest myths and misconceptions. Most of them, unfortunately, are heard and repeated a lot. When you really think them through, though, they have little validity. So now, my friends...on to some mental preparation.

Chapter 4: Mental Preparation

This chapter is all about getting your head screwed on tight, so it doesn't blow off. AKA preparation for the big day!

I know you are chomping at the bit for the actual potty training, but making sure your head is screwed on tight is a very important part of the how-to (actually, it's an important part of parenting, in general).

The very first thing we have to do is to get rid of any notion you might have of how long this process should take. I've already stated my piece about magical three-day training. Yes, it can take a child three days to potty train. It can also take one day. And it can also take seven. I find it very interesting that everyone adores the uniqueness of their children - we love that each one is as different and special as a snowflake - and yet, many parents want a cookie-cutter version of potty training. There's no such thing. It doesn't exist. Also, it infuriates me that your neighbor with two children thinks she knows everything about this potty training gig.

While there are many potty training "methods," there are really only two general systems floating around out there:

1. Rewards
2. Consistency and commitment

That's it.

We are going to work within the second system. Your child is special; she has her very own genetic makeup. She has her very own learning method and speed. We have to honor that, okay? If there were JUST ONE WAY to potty train your child — absolutely guaranteed, no hassles, in three days flat — that crap would be on Oprah (or would've been, anyway). It'd be viral in seconds. We'd all know about it. But we are dealing with **humans**, who react as individuals and have their own — albeit, not exactly logical — thought processes, and who not only know how to push your buttons, they actually installed your buttons.

Using the potty is both one of the first things you actively teach your child, and one of the first things he actively learns. What we are going to discover through this process is how your child thinks. **Having a preconceived notion of how long this will take is going to REALLY, HONESTLY muck things up for you.** You will unwittingly put too much pressure on your child and you will drive yourself insane. Trust me. I know this.

I see people getting tripped up on this all the time. You want to potty train with consistency, and you don't want it to take a year. Realistically, I can tell you it takes most people around 7-10 days. Through all my years of doing this, I've come to believe that there's a truly magical window of about two weeks duration in each child's life during which he will potty train so effortlessly, it's amazing. However, when those two weeks are going to happen for any one kid are anyone's guess, and there's no outward signal as to when they are occurring. So when you hear one of those miraculous stories from your friend/neighbor/sister, they got lucky is all.

Before you actually begin any potty training, you will need to do a few things in preparation for getting started.

Set a date: You need to pick a date to start the process. You can pick any start date. I usually recommend starting about two weeks after reading this book, but really, tomorrow is fine, too. The two week waiting period is to prepare you and to give your mind a break. Chances are, you've been spending a lot of time lately reading up on potty training, thinking about it, asking around the playground, fending off the know-it-alls, and feeling a little guilty every time you change a diaper. Give yourself two weeks to NOT think about it. Set a date that will allow you, and hopefully your partner, to focus fully on potty training for three or four days. Holiday weekends are perfect. This is the same sort of preparation period people go through when they pick a date to start a workout routine, a diet, or to quit smoking. It gives you that last hoorah. Set your date and luxuriate in diapers for those two weeks. The waiting period also preps you for a major transition in your child's life - from baby to little kid. I find some parents have a fear about giving up their baby. It's a bittersweet time and worth self-examination. It's my personal philosophy that we shouldn't try to hold our children back to fill our own emotional needs. In a bit, I'll offer some advice to help both you and your child cope with the emotions of the transition.

Get a potty chair, or if you already have one out, put it in hiding: Every single parent that has attended my class has made the "put the pot out so they can get used to it" mistake. If you haven't put it out, don't. If you have and your child has **only** ever used it to pee and poop in, you may leave it out. If the potty chair has been used for anything else besides peeing and pooping, put it away.

I also don't suggest letting your child pick their own potty chair. They'll inevitably pick one with bells and whistles, and you don't need that. This isn't a toy. Personally, I'm a huge fan of the Baby Bjorn potty chairs. If your child asks to use the potty chair between now and your selected start date, go ahead and let him. So, say you've set a start date for two weeks from now. He's been using the potty, but inconsistently. Still, it's in the bathroom and has not become any sort of toy. You can leave it out. During the two weeks between now and your start date, if he asks to use it, let him. But don't make a big deal about it. Just say, "Thank you for using the potty." You are not going to mention potty training. You are not going to give accolades. Just go with a simple thank you, or a reflection back to him: "You used the potty chair to pee in. Thank you."

Clear your social calendar for a week, starting with your start date: Just to clarify, let's say you've decided to start potty training in two weeks on a Sunday. You will clear your calendar for a week, starting with that Sunday.

I usually crack up at the look on moms' faces when I say this. Jaws drop, faces go white. What?! Yes, clear your calendar for a week. (Don't worry working moms; we'll hit daycare situations in a bit.)

You will be home for the first few days, with small outings planned. After that, you want to be at your child's bathroom beck and call for at least a week. The reason for this calendar-clearing is simple: if you have things planned, you're more likely to get stressed out. What if your child had a lot to drink in the morning and doesn't pee and it's time for *Music Together*, story time at the library, a play date, or whatever? You are more likely to pressure him or get aggravated. You're tempting fate with an accident in the car. What if your child has to poop and you're in the one place that has an out-of-order toilet? At this point, you will only be three days into potty training; you will still have a way to go before you and your child absolutely know his signals. Set yourself and your child up for success!

I'm asking you to clear a small amount of time. I've had parents practically flip out and tell me they can't possibly stay home for a few days, to which I respond that if you can't stay home with your child for a few days, you might want to change your priorities. At this age, your child should be neither over-scheduled nor overstimulated with entertainment. If you and your partner are both full-time workers out of the home, I've got a whole chapter on daycares; that is its own ball of wax. In a full-time daycare situation, it's usually best to pick a three-day holiday weekend, and maybe even take an extra day off to make it a four-day weekend. The more time your child has to learn this with **you**, in the familiar setting of **home**, the better it sticks.

———————————— *Consider This* ————————————

An interesting side note to clearing your calendar: just one generation ago, kids were potty trained at 17-22 months. I truly believe it's because our moms, for the most part, were stay-at-home moms. I mean

*stay at home. They didn't work at home, they had
no computer for email and Facebook, no cell phones,
no identities to preserve, no mommy groups, no
playdates, no baby gymnastics, no music classes and
no swimming lessons. Now, I'm 43, so maybe I'm
talking to a younger audience here, and I'm certainly
not saying our moms exhibited the best parenting.
But I do believe it was that stay-at-home factor that
made potty training so easy. Between my mom and
her three best friends, they literally had 20 kids in a
10 year span. All four moms used cloth diapers, and
none had a dryer. And each of those kids was fully
potty trained by 22 months.*

If there's any pressure for your child to perform, it'll backfire
and have you unnecessarily pulling your hair out. Do yourself
a favor and listen to me. Clear your calendar. Please don't
make the mistake of assuming your child is going to be the
potty training all-star. They exist, but usually where we don't
expect them. Do not think I'm making this up. Many parents
have fallen prey to the fantasy, "My kid is smart, he'll pick
this up. I'm clearing my calendar for three days and then
that's it! Back to business as usual. I don't have time for this
to take longer than that."

Again, trust me. That very thinking will lead to tears — yours.

One week before the big day: Start talking about
throwing away diapers. Don't mention potty training. Don't
mention anything about the toilet or pee or poop. Just

mention as you're changing diapers, "On Sunday, we're going to throw your diapers away." This should be level and calm and very loving. Don't show your nerves and don't make it a big deal. The logic behind this is it's not wrought with anxiety. Who can't throw away a few diapers? Jeez, Mom... that's easy.

This is also a great time to start with big boy/girl talk. Start going through the list of big kid stuff your child does. Kids love hearing about what they can do now that they couldn't do as a baby. This is preparing both you and your child for the end of this baby portion of her life.

This particular phase in your child's life is also a place in which your language can generate a mixed message. See if these sounds familiar:

"Who's my baby?"

"No, honey, that's not for little kids."

"Stop that now, you're a big girl."

So, what is your child: a big kid, a little kid, or a baby?

It may not seem like that big a deal, but being able to recognize and address this will come in handy. Sometimes our big kids need babying, and it's good when they can separate and articulate that. One child I worked with years ago came up with the phrase, "I need some baby love." I thought this was brilliant and adopted it when training my own son. It worked like magic. Kids aren't so afraid of becoming a "big kid" if they know they can have some "baby love" when they need it. Right now, they're in limbo; we know they aren't really big kids, but they aren't babies either. To this day, Pascal asks for "baby love" (actually, he calls it Mama Love, but it means the same). It lasts about 30 seconds, and then he's onto bigger and better "big boy" things. Still, it gives us that infusion of love and snuggles we both crave.

So you've set a date, ideally giving yourself a two-week head start. You've put the potty chair away for now. You've cleared your social calendar for a week. And you've planted the idea, super casual-like, that you are tossing diapers out.

Now...are you done, done? With diapers, I mean?
This is an added section of the book since the first edition because it didn't use to be such a huge problem, largely because we didn't used to have such huge online communities. What's the problem? Self-doubt. On the surface, it doesn't appear to be a problem but in reality, it's the worst kind. It chips away at this process and makes it nearly impossible to potty train. I can always tell when parental self-doubt is the niggling issue underneath a child who "just doesn't seem to be getting it." There are all manner of problems that can arise when you are teaching your child this new skill, but "just not getting it" shouldn't be one of them. If dogs have the capacity to house train in under a week, surely human children can do this as well. If you find yourself saying, or maybe you've already attempted potty training and have said, "He's just not getting it", chances are self-doubt is your problem.

I call it **done**, done.

Are you really ready to potty train your child? Are you done with diapers or are you **done**, done with diapers? I know you are going to say you are done with diapers. But are you **really**?

I find most parents really can't wait to be done with diapers, but I also find those same parents are in two camps regarding the process of potty training their child: sure and unsure. Where are you? Think about this carefully. It's the best indicator of how the process will go for you. Ask yourself a few questions to help determine where you are:

1. Are you going into potty training thinking you'll give it a try and see what happens? We've talked a little about the word "try," but I mean it **for real**: your head can't be in this place. "Trying" to potty train sets a clear expectation that you don't expect it to work. Why try? Instead, why not pretend that I single-handedly managed to blow up every disposable diaper factory. (I dream big. Naturally this takes place while I'm clad in a black latex cat suit.) There are no more diapers. Of course, I'm joking...kind of. Don't give yourself a wimpy start with, "We're going to try." In fact, if you plan to "try," don't bother starting. It's not going to happen if you try. It will happen when you **do**. Remember Yoda. Do or do not. There is no try.

2. Are you unsure that your child is ready? Are you worried that she's too young? Most of the first chapters in this book are to reassure you that it is not only possible but **preferable** to potty train when your child is younger. But if you still think your child is too young or somehow not capable, the process will be an epic failure for you.

'Ready' is a nebulous a concept. It's better to ask yourself, "Is my child CAPABLE of doing this?" Answer this question deep in your own gut. Everyone around you is going to have an opinion, I assure you. **Don't listen to everyone else**. Listen to what your heart says about your child.

3. Why do you want your child to potty train? This is a tricky one. Be honest with yourself. Yes, pretty much every parent wants to be done with diapers. That's an okay motivator, but not a great one. It's like eating healthy to lose weight. You have to have a stronger motivator than that or it crumbles under pressure. Also, look really deep inside. When I first met former client "Elizabeth," it was because this whole process had fallen apart for her. She did everything by the book. Also, her child's learning curve was slow. She admitted — in a very vulnerable way, which I truly admire — that she was embarrassed. She wanted to be the first of her friends to potty train and it wasn't going well for her. That wasn't the only reason the process fell apart but it put a pretty powerful crack in it. Don't potty train right now because you want an all-star. Without fail, you won't have one. Don't do this to prove anyone wrong.

    What *is* a good reason to potty train your child? Well, to give him self-esteem and self-pride in mastering of a skill. My **favorite** kind of thank you — and I hear it often — goes something like this: "I just LOVE the look on my daughter's face. She is SO proud of herself." I say it over and over: you don't hand your child self-esteem. She develops it by mastering tasks. **That** is a great motivator!

4. What do all your friends and immediate family think of you potty training? This is **huge**. If every day is a battle for you — all the people in your close circle are jamming down your throat that your kid is too young — you are going to have massive doubts. Potty train anyway, but be sure you get your head on tight beforehand and keep it there during the process. Perhaps don't hang out with any friends for a week.

I cannot tell you how much a doubting circle of friends and family damages your resolve. I originally tried to potty train Pascal at 18 months, because I know it's absolutely possible to do at that age. I'm a single mom, and at that time, I owned a store, and knew his daycare wasn't on board with my plans. I knew within the first 4 hours of our first day of potty training that it wasn't 'clicking' easily for him. I realized potty training him at that time was still possible, but that it would take longer than a couple of days. I abandoned ship and he did just fine at 22 months. The **only** reason I'm telling you this story is because my circle of "friends" at this time couldn't wait to gloat. I'm serious! "See, told you so." I phased them out of my life in short order. Screw that. For real. You should be able to potty train your child without everyone coming down on you. "If only I could potty train on a deserted island for two weeks, I'd be fine," is a sentiment I hear often from clients. Don't let the naysayers get you down. I don't know why, but this is an area where people feel very free to tell you exactly what you're doing wrong. It's bizarre to me. Nobody would dream of telling you how to discipline your children, right?

I think the problem of the naysayers has a deeper level, too. If you potty train your kid successfully, then the people who said you couldn't do it look like lame-Os. And you've just kicked their parenting advice to the mat. In other words, they have an emotional investment in your failure. So be wary of well-meaning friends who tell you your child is too young. Or that you are doing it wrong. Or that you should just give your kid a freaking piece of candy every time she poops. Question these folks outright if you're feeling brave. "Why are you so invested in when I potty train my child?"

Plus — I know this from Facebook — in short order, you are going to be gloating **your** butt off. But just don't go into potty training with that as the sole purpose, okay?

If you breezed through those last 4 questions, go back and ask yourself again. Be sure you are ready to **do** this. Be confident that your child not only has the capability to do it, but that he but will blossom in this new-found skill. Potty train for the right reasons - because it's time, because it's the next developmental milestone, and, yeah, maybe to stick it to Big Diaper. Be sure you have support around you or avoid the people who don't support you.

I really can't express how important those points are! Yes, it's okay to be a little nervous. Some people have made potty training into a huge ordeal, largely because they waited too long and now do have real disasters on their hands. In the majority of cases, though, it's just not that big a deal. Sure, it's okay to have a tiny pocket of concern or doubt. Just don't go in with the pocket of doubt leading the show. I see this time and time and time again, and your child absorbs his attitude toward potty training from you. Whether you call it "vibe" or "energy" or "non-verbal cues," the fact of the matter is that children absorb our energy. They feel the emotional undercurrent of any given situation. Your child can tell if you are sad even when you're putting on your happy face. Your child is extremely sensitive; all kids are. They don't have the layers of emotional armor we've piled on ourselves so as not to be so vulnerable. **They will feel your vibe**.

If you are doubting, they will be doubting, and the result will look like they're 'not getting it.' If your prevailing thoughts are, "I'm not sure she's ready," guess what? It's going to look like she's not ready, or ' not getting it.' Expectations, and therefore outcomes, will be very unclear. She'll be getting mixed messages from you and they will confuse her. She won't have the words to say, "Hey Mom, I'm getting two different things from you right now. I'm not sure what I'm doing here." Instead, she just 'won't get it' as far as the potty training goes. If your mouth is saying one thing and your heart is saying another, she will be confused. Make sense?

Now for a few major modern day issues that need to be addressed. These aren't questions and answers, per se, but addressing these issues is definitely in the "get your head screwed on tight" category.

Nix the Facebook status. For now: For the love of all that is holy; please do not post on Facebook that you are starting potty training. When you are done, post away. Make it your status every day for a freaking year, if you want! But if you post about **starting** potty training, you will immediately get at least 34 comments from all kinds of "experts." I'm really glad your best friend used candy to potty train her kid but, but **you** know better. Well-meaning friends are going fill you with doubt. If you are experiencing troubles or doubts or just want to bitch, join us on the Oh Crap Potty Training Facebook page, where you'll find like-minded mamas and lots of good support. Don't expect that on your personal Facebook page.

Sleep: Yes, we are moms. We are the legions of the under-rested. I'm talking about you, but more importantly, I'm talking about your child. Our children as a whole are grossly sleep deprived. A two-year-old needs around 12 hours of sleep a day, and most don't get anywhere near that much. The craziest thing about sleep is that a tired kid acts like a wired kid. So when it's around 7 in the evening, and you think your kid isn't tired because he's chasing the dog around in circles, you're likely wrong. That kid is probably overtired. Another important sign of an overtired kid is if bedtime is a fiasco. Bedtime shouldn't be a hassle. If it is, chances are your child is overtired. Overtired kids are clumsier, have more freak outs and tantrums, 'poke' at others and are generally fussier. "No I waaaant the pink cup. No. The blue cup. No. The pink cup." You know the drill. Of course, toddlers are known for their fickleness, but tired kids tend to go above and beyond with regard to the crazy. **Fix sleep**

before beginning potty training. Always, always go for **more** sleep. An excellent book is *Sleepless In America* by Mary Sheedy Curcinka. She's compassionate about your child's needs, specifically with regard to the need for more sleep. I've thoroughly enjoyed her take on the problem and the suggestions in her book. I'm not going to spend a whole lot of time talking about sleep, but you really want this duck in the row before you begin.

Potty train the kid you have: This is a good one. You have the kid you have, not necessarily the kid you want. You cannot change your zebra's stripes. This is hard for us to admit, and hard to remember. We all want the well-behaved, loving, courteous child. But we got what we got. And no matter what, our love is fierce. While you are potty training, be careful not to linger in the "I wish he..." fantasy world. Deal with the kid and the problems you have. Your fantasies are irrelevant. Your kid comes with all his own crazy, his own stuff, his own DNA. There's a lot of 'nature' in this here 'nurture.' The goal is always to work with your child's strengths. While working with a client, I never try to 'fix' a perceived weakness. We build on what your kid inherently has.

There's another aspect to making sure you're potty training "the kid you have". If your child has a particular 'problem' before you start potty training — say he's whiny, or she's resistant, or he's prone to histrionics and tantrums — you are going to have that same kid and the same problem while you are potty training. That's not a judgment. All these behaviors are normal, and there's not a single one I have not seen. The behavior isn't the real issue, in fact. The real problem is when parents somehow convince themselves that potty training is going to happen in a bubble, that **all** the other behavior your child typically exhibits is somehow going to disappear while you are potty training. Not only will it still be there - it may even get magnified for a short time. Again, it's all good. Just keep your expectations level.

Pants, clothing and independence: Does your child dress herself? You might want to get started teaching this skill, if your child doesn't already possess it. I find it's something we don't even really think about until we start potty training, and then it's like AHHHH!

───────────── *From the Blog* ─────────────

Yay! More and more parents are choosing to ditch the diapers at around 18-20 months. For most kids, it's so easy at this age. BUT a lot of kids don't yet know how to manipulate their clothing. Nothing is more frustrating to you OR your child than knowing he has to pee and making the move to the pot, only to get tied up in mangled attempts to get his pants down. Ahhhhh!

A few things can help. First off, who the heck started saying PULL your pants down? Toddlers are very literal. While teaching them how to use their pants, use the words PUSH your pants down. That's really what they're doing, right?

Definitely, start having your child dress themselves. This, in and of itself, is huge. It gives them such empowerment! It also makes for some massive skill-building. When you are teaching your child to dress herself, it can sometimes require a few more words than, "I'm putting your pants on". Remember, this is a brand new skill to her! So really break down what you are doing: "I'm hooking my thumb into the elastic, see? And then I can grab them and push them down."

Some parents have found a 'dressing party' has helped. Much like playing dress up clothes, spend an hour trying on outfits. Make it seem fun! Practice is the key here, and most kids at this age don't get a whole lot of practice. And the pressure of a looming need to pee doesn't make for the best learning, either. So set up some teaching time to, literally and figuratively, get the pants down.

And some of you may think I'm a whack job and way over-thinking things. But I can't tell you how frustrating it is to be this close to consistent pee in the potty and have the damn pants mess you up!

This is also a good time to really start fostering some independence and setting some expectations. Have a set chore for your child, like putting his dish in the sink after dinner. This makes your child feel big and independent, but also envelops him in a feeling of being part of the whole. They **love** having and knowing their place in your home.

Dads/partners: This is a doozy!

Please be sure your partner is on board with this whole process. This is easier if you get them on board **before** you begin. At the end of the book, there is a "Dads' Cheat Sheet." I'm saying "dads" for ease, but other moms, partners or anyone else who shares caregiving fit in this category. This can include moms if dad is the primary caregiver.

Now, I want to be super clear here. I am making some huge generalizations based on my work in the real world. This entire section is not meant to alienate ANY partners who are reading this. If you ARE reading this, you are awesome. I've been told some dads feel left out and pandered to in this chapter and I apologize. Please realize there are masses of dads who aren't fully engaged in parenting. It's been such a problem in the past that I simply can't leave it without addressing it. Thank you for your understanding.

Some partners really love reading the book and getting involved, and some don't. A really good sign your partner isn't on board is if they won't read this book (or at least, parts of it). I'm telling you straight up, this is going to be a problem.

I think there are a couple of reasons some dads don't jump at the opportunity to potty train. I think one of the major ones is that they aren't used to doing the bulk of the potty-related work. Often, they didn't change the majority of the diapers, and they don't expect to be the major potty trainer. It's a common joke that men won't stop for directions. Well, consider this book 'directions.' And for a guy who doesn't want to ask for help, advice might be unwelcome. Period.

Also, the majority of dads are working, and I suspect that many come home and want to be the "good guy". Further, they are tired and cranky themselves, so containing crap is not their idea of fun. I get it. But remind them this is **temporary**.

Some men are super-linear thinkers and don't really connect with the chaos of the toddler mind. I can't tell you how many times I've seen a situation like this: Mom's been working her butt off to potty train the kid during the day. She leaves the child in her husband's care for 20 minutes. The child has an accident. Mom asks Dad what happened and he says, "I told him to go and he said no." I think dads really expect that you only have to tell your child that he needs to pee in the potty one time and the child should fully comprehend and comply.

If you sense resistance from your mate, try to get to the bottom of it before you begin. If you begin with a recalcitrant mate, potty training becomes straight up crazy. You'll spend your time battling and trying to prove yourself rather than teaching your child to use the toilet. This process of proving yourself to your mate will undermine your success by putting you on edge. It will also put a **ton** of pressure on your child, which will backfire on you.

Particular areas of resistance include that some dads honestly and truly believe the child is too young. After all, the (weird) norm right now in our country is protracted diaper-wearing, and delayed potty training, so you may be battling against your partner's perception of what's "normal" or "right" if you want to potty train right now. Add to this that some dads think rewards are good, and as we've already discussed, this is reward-free potty training. Then there are the people who just can't commit to a process and be consistent. They tend to be wary of any one process or book, and think there's something better out there. I've had many a dad question my process. One went out and bought two more books. Only after reading them did he come to realize I kind of have a good thing here.

So, say you have flat-out refusal to participate or you are sensing some resistance. First off, don't ignore it! Yes, you may have a child who's an all-star and you can laugh in your mate's face in a couple of days and do the "nah, nah, nah, nah," dance soon enough. But my experience is that when one of the parents isn't into this, the process goes awry with your child. She's got two different energetic forces coming at her, and she'll be confused. Also, don't expect your partner to just 'stay out of your way'. The problem is, unless your partner is gone for significant chunks of time, he will get in your way at some point. Your child is also destined to be in his care at some point.

What you can do is try to have a heart-to-heart in a down moment — after sex if you can arrange it. Kidding. Kind of. I mean don't try to talk about it when there's chaos, like at dinner or bedtime. Try to get at what's really under his resistance. Bring up the various points I've mentioned. Ask him outright. Don't let him get away with vague answers. If he has a real, honest, legitimate objection, that's something you two need to discuss further and work out.

If you suspect he's just not interested because he's probably not the one doing the work...not good enough. I think sometimes we, as moms, trample on dads because we are the primary caregivers (huge generalization, but you know what I mean). I've had dads that, as it turns out, were just hurt that the mom went and decided to tackle a huge milestone without his input. He's vital to this process, just as you are, so let's involve him right from the beginning. And let's understand and validate how he truly feels about this process, yeah?

Oh, and when your kid **is** potty trained, you can expect Dad to practically explode with pride and lap up the congratulations. Seriously.

A word about potty chairs: It's a pretty good idea to have a little potty chair, even if you are morally opposed to them. We really want to foster independence. Your child most likely is a long way away from being able to manage the big toilet alone, even with a step-stool. The potty chair is temporary; soon, he will be big enough for the "regular" toilet. I am a fan of both potty chairs and inserts for the big toilet. I have no opinion whatsoever about where you keep the potty chair or how many you have around the house. Buy a pot for every room if you want. I wouldn't worry about any sort of bathroom etiquette at this point. I know some parents feel strongly about only doing poop or pee in the bathroom but personally, I don't think it matters. Children need the convenience of a close-by potty. Privacy and bathroom etiquette will come naturally with time.

I will, however, point you toward **this**: The Squatty Potty. It is the most amazing product ever. You may want to look into buying one as a extra step-stool for the bathroom. I'll talk more about that in the poop chapter.

Potty training a nursing toddler: If you are still nursing, right on! That's awesome. The approach to potty training won't be any different, but there is one little twist: because you don't know exactly how much is going in, you have to be a little more alert as to when it comes out. I have to be honest though; in my observations, breastmilk doesn't act like "just" a beverage in the toddler body. It seems to count as food, as far as the body is concerned. Here's what this means: if your child drinks 10oz of water or juice, you can be pretty certain you're going to get at least 6oz of pee out at some point. With breastmilk, the math is not the same. Do not try to wean your child right before or during potty training! Potty training is a big transition, and your child won't emotionally be able to handle both at the same time. Plus, she may need the stability and comfort of your breast while acclimating to this other big new thing.

Precious rugs, floors or furniture: Most people I know with toddlers don't have much that's truly precious. If you do have rooms with expensive oriental rugs or items of furniture that cost more than your house, don't potty train in these rooms. Or make them off-limits for a while. You will freak out when your child pees or poops on these, and there's no greater stall in potty training than a parental freak out. *Casual* is the key word here. Many parents — mostly renters or wooden floor people — confine their child to the kitchen for a day, or just until the child gets the basics down.

So those are the major issues you have to tackle to get and keep your head screwed on tight. Once you are clear on those points, believe me...this process is going to go so much more smoothly! Go back and read the chapter again, if you have to. It's worth getting the steps to mental preparation nailed down before proceeding. Once you've got your mind prepared, take a deep breath and cue up the music from *Jaws*: dundundundun...

Chapter 5: Ditch the Diapers! The How-To

So, you've done your mental prep. Your head is screwed on tight. You've cleared your calendars and you are ready to ditch the diapers.

Remember the timeline. We are taking your child's awareness from **Clueless** to **I Peed** to **I'm Peeing** to **I Have to go Pee**.

This timeline is potty training in a nutshell. That's it! (hahahaha!)

I want you to think of potty training as being made up of blocks of learning. I'm going to call them just that: blocks or phases. No matter where you are starting from, you need to think of the potty training process as a tower of blocks that you are building. If one block is not learned properly, the tower will be unstable and will tumble. Thinking in this way makes potty training so much more approachable. Breaking potty training down into blocks like this will also give you a really good idea of where and when things went wrong if there are any struggles later on. Parents who don't break potty training into blocks and have struggles often don't know where it went wrong. With the block approach, you can say something like, "Oh! He had block one down pat. It was only when we moved to block two that he started struggling." This is extremely helpful for troubleshooting. Because our kids aren't robots, there are all kinds of emotions, behaviors and actual gaps in learning that can really muck up the final goal. The block method allows us to separate these things out from one other so we can figure out what's causing the problem. As a bonus, potty training doesn't look as overwhelming when we think about it in small chunks.

Here are the major blocks or phases, in order:

1. Peeing and pooping while naked, either with prompting or without.
2. Peeing and pooping with clothes on, commando, with prompting or without.
3. Peeing and pooping in different situations, with prompting or without.
4. Peeing and pooping with underpants, with prompting or without.
5. Consistent self-initiation.
6. Night and nap (unless you are choosing to do it all together; more on that later.)
7. College. Probably still needing to occasionally prompt.

I am going to walk you through each block and tell you **how** to do it and **what** you should be looking for. I'll give you some suggestions and few heads-up about specific potential problems. A more complete list of problems will be addressed in later chapters. I don't want to muck up the how-to by discussing every potential problem right up front because many, many parents breeze right through this without a hitch. Okay, ready?

Your Start Date, Block One:

I used to recommend that you make this day a really big deal. I used to suggest junky food and lots of juice and a really fun atmosphere. But over the last few years, I've changed my mind. It used to seem that kids loved a day out of routine, but more recently, it seems that such a deviation from the norm puts kids on high-alert. I also have amended the junky food recommendation. I started potty training before I was a mom and I thought sugar highs were kind of cute in other people's kids. Now that I'm a mom, though — and kind of a health food-nut— I no longer find the sugar highs cute, nor do I think the junk food is necessary.

We want potty training to be the new norm for your child, and the best way to do that is to normalize the process as much as possible for her. That's why we don't want the potty training start day to be so crazy and out-of-routine that it fills your kid with unease. I also have a theory that life these days is just moving too fast. As a result, I think all of our kids are getting anxious, in general. I think the economy and politics and all these grown up concerns are wiring our kids in a huge, 'collective consciousness' way. I think there are many issues associated with this collective vibe even if we, as individuals, do our best to combat it. But really, that's another book entirely.

For now, let's just say that it's best to begin the potty training process with both you and your child as even-keeled and level as possible. To that end, I suggest you start with as little fanfare as possible, so that you **normalize** this process as much as is humanly possible. Using the toilet is just something we all do as socialized beings. I want to remind you here, peeing and pooping are primal behaviors. You don't have to teach your child **how** to pee or poop. Through potty training, you are simply teaching your child **where** to put his waste. Putting his waste in an appropriate container is **socialized**. And our particular society, the appropriate container is a toilet.

Here we go! To begin the first block of learning, take the diaper off your child. If you want, you can make a show of throwing the rest of the diapers away, or you can simply say, "Today, you are going to be a big girl and put your pee and poop in the potty. I'm going to teach you and help you learn this. Yay! It's very fun". You don't have to use those exact words, but you want to state what's happening very clearly, and you want to sound like it's cool. Think of how you would say, "Today, we're going to the dentist," and try to hit the same tone. You want to sound cool and casual, and avoid any hint that you anticipate drama. Clear. Succinct. Direct. Don't ask her opinion about this. Don't ask, "Okay?" In fact, don't **ask** anything. We don't want to give her the opportunity to say no.

You will be home **all day today**. Your child will be **naked all day**. Now, many people tell me their child hates to be naked. Be that as it may, you really do need to have your child bottomless, at the very least. Much of the day is going to consist of you catching your child mid-pee and getting him to the potty. If he has any covering on his bum, by the time you see the pee, it will be too late — his bladder will have emptied. The other benefit to keeping your child naked today is that you will be more likely to see her signals when she is naked. Every kid gives some sort of signal right before she pees. It may be very subtle, but it's there.

I suggest extra fluids today. Usually a couple of juice boxes will do the trick. I'm not a fan of juice boxes, but they're great for this first block of learning. You can also have melon, other fruits, and ice pops. These all count as fluids.

If your child is under 24 months, you should not push extra fluids. I have no idea why, but kids under 24 months can't handle the extra intake. Just give normal amounts of liquid to these little ones.

The idea behind the extra fluid is to get a bit of practice in. Normally, your child may pee around five times a day. We want to bump that up a bit, just temporarily.

A word of caution: if your child is sucking down fluids — I mean, like a ridiculous amount — it will backfire on you. His system will be so out-of-whack that he won't be able to do any serious learning. If this starts to happen, slow down with the extra liquid.

Elisa's mom, a former client, contacted me almost in tears. The first day of potty training, Elisa went gangbusters on the fluids and pretty much was peeing as she was drinking. While it made for a funny visual, this is too much liquid. Look for the happy medium. We want more fluid than usual, but not tons. All we are looking for is pee practice.

Now, let me assure you, this is going to be the most exhausting day of your life. No, I'm serious. Your job today is to **do nothing but watch your child**. If this sounds unbearable, remember the pot of gold at the end of the rainbow! Still, I cannot stress this enough: **TODAY YOU WILL DO NOTHING BUT WATCH YOUR CHILD!**

Have fun projects planned. Play trains and dolls and puzzles. Watch videos, read stories, dance around naked. Let the dishes go, don't vacuum or dust, don't do laundry. You will be on your child like white on rice. No computer! Don't get on the phone! Don't read a magazine or book!

I can't tell you how many parents tell me it went wrong from the first day. "She just peed on the floor." I'll go through the day with them and learn that Mom just 'had to' get on the phone because of this, that, or the other thing, or 'had to' check her email. You have to watch your child and help her get to the potty. She is not yet able to pick up on her need to pee without your help. If there is some pressing matter in your life — someone's in the hospital, you're on call, etc — **then don't pick this day to potty train**!

One way to make this exhausting day sound easier in your own mind is to think of it as a great bonding opportunity. For me personally, after the first day of potty training, I felt closer to my son than I had in months. I felt a bond akin to that of breastfeeding again. Let's face it; around 18 months our kids start showing some independence and we're thrilled! For the first time since birth, we can sit for a moment and maybe read an article with a cup of coffee. We very rarely watch every move our child makes. The house has been child-proofed, he can walk without killing himself and we get a breather. Think of this day as a special opportunity to reconnect. I remember being surprised. There were all these little things he would do that I hadn't seen. Also, I figured out what was happening to all the damn Legos (stacked way under the couch cushions; who knew he had a secret stash?)

One mom reported to me, "We had SUCH a blast that first day! It was almost decadent to get to stay home and just focus on him all day and not rush around doing things. We played all kinds of games, it was just so fun and he did so great. I was so impressed with him!" What I really loved about this mom was how impressed she was by her son, though the way I see things, it took both of them working together to make that first day of potty training successful.

Let's break this day down into minutia, starting with that first pee. If you're doing your job, **which is watching your child**, you'll catch that pee quickly. Don't panic, don't scream. Just say something like, "Oo, oo, hold it honey..." Pick your child up and get him to the potty ASAP. Hopefully, you'll make it in time for some of the pee to go in the pot (yes, you will leave a trail of pee behind). Once the pee is in the pot, you have lots of options, depending on your child. You can high five, dance around, have him look at it and empty it, you can make a big deal out of it, or you can just say, "Thank you" or "Wow. You did it." Don't make the rush to the pot frantic or scary — just quick. I suggest keeping the potty nearby at all times.

You are not to ask you child if she has to go. Never, in the coming week, will you ask your child if she has to go. You will prompt her by saying something like, "Come. It's time to pee."

So, back to that first pee. Honestly, I've seen greater success from parents who wait for the first pee to start and then run the kid to the pot than from parents who randomly sit the kid on the pot to try to pee. Do you understand the difference?

Some people maintain that if you just put your child on the pot every half hour or so, eventually they'll pee. A lot of daycares train this way. It can work, but I've found it's more effective to wait for the child to start peeing and then get him to the toilet. I think this is because he makes the connection between "feeling" and "doing" faster this way. Just sitting on the potty and waiting for the pee doesn't allow him to connect the dots as fast.

Over the course of the next few pees, one of two things will happen: either your child won't recognize that he's peeing (still 'clueless'), or your child will notice that he's peed or he's peeing. Most kids skip directly to the "I'm peeing" stage, which is typically characterized by a funny look on his face. This look is part interest — there's a certain fascination for him in watching himself pee, to be sure — but he'll also probably look at you like a deer in the headlights. "Uh-oh... what the hell am I supposed to do now?" Keep an eye out for this look. Often it comes right before the pee, and it can help you get your child to the toilet in time.

The first day proceeds. By the third pee, she'll probably know it's coming 1-2 seconds before it actually starts. Rush to the potty. Each time she pees, she'll know a little further in advance, which will buy you a bit more time to get her to the potty. Watching your child closely this first day will also give you an idea of what kind of pee-er you have. Some kids do five little pees after taking in some fluid, others wait an hour and then do one huge pee.

Being naked, your child may very quickly catch on and sit by himself. A quick note about boys: definitely have him sit down to pee for now. Hold his penis down for him and tell him what you're doing to teach him how. Don't have him attempt standing and aiming yet.

Somewhere in Block One, you should start to get good at noticing 'that look' in your child's eyes, which is generally accompanied by some sort of physical signal that you'll begin to recognize. You may see him stand perfectly still, or stop playing. He may or may not signal with his hands and/or words. When you see the look and/or signal, help him get to the potty. Are you seeing how this day works? Again, with all the fluids he's drinking, there should be a fair number of pees. Even if your child is a camel, though, remember: no asking if he has to go. Just prompt him every so often. Expect success. Most kids I've worked with 'get it' remarkably fast. You may even be getting a few seconds heads-up that the pee is coming.

The first several pees may not go in the exact order described here. It may take your child a few pees before you get that extra second or so of warning. Just remember the general idea is to increase your child's awareness to the point that she can tell you before she has to go.

If you're not seeing this progression of awareness, it's okay. I repeat: it's okay. It's really hard to determine how well things are going in these first few days. It's very common to have what looks like a disaster in the first two or three days, and then have things magically click into place. Still, if you're worried that there is no progress, it's worth taking a minute to check in with yourself. Are you truly watching your child, or have you gotten distracted? Are you making too big a deal of all this? There is a delicate balance between prompting and backing off. Remember, potty training should be an effort for you, but not for your child. Are you hounding her? In your child's mind, today should be about special one-on-one time with Mom and/or Dad, and learning a new skill. Don't let drama and your nervousness take over. Children resist when there's too much pressure. As with parenting in general, in potty training if you are met with resistance, you must examine your own actions. I'm not placing blame, it's just that sometimes we don't realize the pressure we're putting on our kids. Remember, pressure can be either verbal or non-verbal, and kids are masters at picking up your non-verbal cues.

Few, if any, kids go straight from this first day of potty training into telling you with words that they have to pee or poop. This is important to remember. A lot of parents expect that the verbal indication will happen sooner than it does, and are befuddled by the number of accidents their child has. From start date to self-initiation usually takes about three weeks for most kids, even super-verbal communicators.

As for that first poop, remember how weird it is going to feel to your child, who is used to pooping in a diaper. My advice, as with pee, is to wait for it to come rather than using the 'sitting and trying' routine. Signals of an impending poop to watch for are an intense look of concentration, grunting, twitching, indicating physical discomfort, rubbing the belly, sudden crankiness, and retreating to a corner, under the table, or some private place. You then put your child on the pot. I really do suggest the little pot; the squat used to sit down will help ease the poop out. Have wipes/TP handy, grab a favorite book or two, and get comfortable. Read the stories to your child. If he grunts and screws up his face, just grunt along with him. Without over-talking, you can softly offer encouragement (I say softly because this is sort of an inward function). "It's coming, you can do it. Uhh. Go ahead honey, let it out."

Encourage, but don't pressure. If your child gets freaked out and starts to cry, keep her on the pot and just hug her. Look her in the eye if that helps her — some kids really need you to look them in the eye if they're having a hard time, though when things are progressing normally, most kids prefer not to be stared down — and let her know it's okay. If she's having trouble it could be that the poop is hard, or she could just be freaked out. For the first few poops — most kids will go down to pooping once a day — you may have to read to her for a while. That's normal. Also, this is a suggestion I'll mention throughout the book that you can start with the first poop, so it becomes routine: put some thick books under your child's feet. We want her thighs as close to her chest as possible. This will mimic the squat position she knows and loves. It also physically helps the poop come out better.

Have your child carry the little pot to dump in the big toilet. This is the reward. Let me tell you, most kids will **love** it! He'll be so proud and amazed at this poop, as well he should be. If it works for your child, give him more verbal praise and high fives. I also recommend helping your child connect "feeling" with "doing". "Wow, your belly must feel GOOD after that HUGE poop!" I've found that kids respond well to adjectives and exclamations like, "huge," "tons," "wow," "my goodness," etc. — basically anything with an exclamation point!

Praise: There are a few different theories on praise. Some parents don't believe in praising at all. They'd rather have their child develop an inner sense of pride than depend upon external reinforcement. I personally think a "good job" once in a while is fine, though in my own parenting I try not to say it over and over just for something to say. If you don't feel comfortable praising your child, you can always "reflect" back to them with no judgement. This would look like, "Oh. You peed on the floor," or "You peed in the potty." Either praising or reflecting is fine. I do think, since there really is only one desirable outcome, that there should be **something** in your voice that says 'Yay' this or 'No' that. This often gets overlooked if you are someone who doesn't want to praise. You do have to let your child know, in some manner, that peeing on the floor is 'not good' and on the potty is 'good.' I don't recommend those words, but you must find a way to convey the notion because otherwise, you're teaching your child that it's ok to pee wherever, which is not what potty training is about. I'm particularly fond of having the parent say, "You did it," and/or having the child say, "I did it!" This gives the success over to your child as theirs and, for some kids, has more impact than standard praise or mirroring.

Poop: Poop is a huge deal. HUGE. So huge, it's got its own chapter (the longest chapter in this book, actually). For now, though, let's just address the single biggest poop question I get, which is what to do if you missed the poop or your child didn't poop at all on the first day of potty training.

Most kids show some sort of sign that they are about to poop, but some can drop it like it's hot. If you miss the poop that first day, it's okay — the whole process doesn't fall apart. Get back on the horse. Don't let it undermine your confidence. Clean it up and say something simple and to the point. This is where reflecting back to the child is really helpful: "You pooped on the floor. Poop goes in the potty. Sit on the potty to poop." Simple and direct. You don't want to scold your child on this first day, but it's very important that you communicate in tone, voice, and body language what you expect. This concept is brand new, and your child needs to learn the rules of the game. Don't use the words, "It's okay" if poop ends up on the floor. For some kids, those specific words imply permission.

If your child doesn't poop at all on this first day, or if she normally poops in the morning and doesn't today, it's okay. Again, we'll be looking at poop very closely soon enough. Pooping behavior generally changes during potty training. When wearing a diaper, most children poop as many as three or more times a day. During potty training, that typically goes down to about one poop a day. I don't know why this is. I suspect it's a natural consolidation and part of socialization. I mean, who has time to sit and poop three times a day, you know?

Anyway, if your child doesn't poop (or doesn't poop at the normal time) today, it's nothing to be concerned with. As for holding poop, yes, it can be uncomfortable, but medically speaking a child can go two weeks without a poop before most pediatricians will even blink. Your child is in no danger if he holds it for a day or two. I want to remind you again that your vibe is running the show. If you are freaked out or overly anxious about getting a poop out of your child, he will hold it. The best thing to do is to act super casual and assume the poop is (eventually) coming.

A few notes about "accidents" in Block One. Any pee/poop that ends up on the floor is not an accident at this point; it's a learning tool. Have your child help clean up and don't scold her. Use positive but simple language. "You are learning. You pooped on the floor. Next time, your poop goes in the potty."

Another thing many parents don't know is that pee is sterile. You can drink your own pee. I know...why would you want to? But you can. A quick tangent: I used to be a trapeze artist. We would regularly lose big areas of skin on our hands and legs to the bar. The fastest way to heal? Pee on it. I'm not kidding. Pee would heal up the skin in about a day. I performed with a girl who saved her pee and would bathe in it. Gross, right? Her skin was flawless though. All by way of saying, yes, there really are freaky circus people and no, you don't have to be afraid of pee.

Okay, now it's nap time on day one. You will still use diapers for naps (and bedtime), but you will now clearly and directly tell your child what is going on: "I'm going to put a diaper on you for nap because you're still learning. You've done such a good job today and your nap is a long time. You may not remember to pee when you're sleeping. When you wake up, we're going to take it right off."

You've stated it clearly so your child knows to expect and why. No child I have ever worked with has ever questioned this. It's like they know they'll be asleep and not in control of things. I've also never had a child bring up the fact that just four hours ago we made a big deal of throwing out said diapers. I would make sure to have a go at a pee before a nap.

I used to suggest holding off on the nap if you hadn't gotten a poop in the morning hours. This is ultimately your call, as you know your child's routine best. If you suspect a poop is brewing, you can slightly delay the nap, but I've come to the conclusion that having a tired child is the quickest way to derail potty training. So don't hold off on the nap for too long. We need your child rested. If he does poop in the naptime diaper, it's okay for the moment. If it becomes a habit we will have to deal with it, but for the first few days it's okay. Typically, the child isn't holding the poop in specifically for the nap diaper. Rather, there's been a lot to learn, and as he relaxes during sleep, the poop just comes naturally.

After nap, continue on with the day the way it's been. You'll probably be exhausted. That's normal. Your child may be exhausted. That's also okay. Your kid's had to learn a lot about something she paid no attention to until a short while ago. Many children may seem more needy or clingy. If you are still nursing, your child will probably want to nurse more. This is all okay and expected.

I wouldn't put any sort of thought into whether the nap/ bedtime diapers are wet or dry. If your child has shown progress during the day, a wet diaper means nothing. As your child gets better at holding it till he reaches the pot, he will naturally start staying dry. The good news is this happens in a short period of time. I will address actual night training at the end of this chapter. Also, in the beginning phases of potty training, he may not yet be fully emptying his bladder, so nap and night diapers may be more full than usual. This evens out with time and practice.

If you intend to give up all diapers, even for naps and nighttime, be sure to read the beginning of the *Night Training* chapter. It's actually a better way to potty train, but I understand that it can look overwhelming to attempt.

If you partake in alcohol, please have some wine at the end of this day. It is also acceptable to have wine in your cereal when potty training. You deserve it.

After this first day of potty training, you should have a relatively good idea of when and how often your child needs to use the potty. More importantly, your child should have a relatively good idea of when, where, and how to pee.

Chances are Block One has either left you elated or bummed. You may be stoked that you and your child both have a good handle on this potty training thing, or you may be feeling like your child absolutely didn't get it. If you're feeling like this first day didn't prove so successful, examine where and when things might have gotten tripped up. Check in and be honest with yourself on what you may have done to hamper the process. I really encourage you to look at your own behavior during potty training rather than putting it solely on your child. Many parents have told me their child is too intense, too stubborn, or too something, but — and I say this without judgment — usually these parents tend to be the same. So not only have the parents passed this trait on to the child, but they (the parents) act this way during the process of potty training. Know your own style, and be willing to adjust accordingly. Try to strike the careful balance of being extremely attentive without being over-reactive or overbearing.

At this point I also feel it's worth mentioning a particular phenomenon I see as a mom and as a potty trainer. Parenting has gotten oddly competitive in a strange way. Most of us know it's not healthy to push our children to see who can read sooner and who can spell or do whatever else better. Still, there's an odd thing happening that I don't even think most parents are aware of, which is a sort of reverse competitiveness. It's as though parents are competing to have the child who is most special because of a negative: he refuses sleep, she's always sick, he's so intense, she's never done what everyone else does, he never lets me eat, and so on. Please don't make your child special for not potty training. It's an area where it's just fine to be average. In fact, go in the other direction. If your kid's going to be special, let him be special for doing it quickly and easily.

In any event, should you feel your child really hasn't gotten the gist of potty training after the first day, that's okay. Our 24 hour system dictates that you move on to day two, but it's totally fine if you're still in Block One as far as learning goes. Blocks are defined by progress made, not by time passed. I can't state this enough: **every child is different**. Remember that timeline we talked about? **Clueless** to **I peed** to **I'm peeing** to **I have to pee**? Look for progress, not perfection. Nothing is really a problem on these first few days. It's vital to remember how new this is to your child. We cannot expect them to 'get it' just because we say it, and this whole thing is a process, okay? If they need a little more time on Block One, that's fine.

For subsequent days in Block One, you will go back to normal fluid consumption and work on getting the pee in the potty.

END RESULT: A successful completion of Block One should look something along the lines of your child, while naked, can sit to pee and poop on the potty. This can be because you prompted, you led him, or he went on his own. **If you do not see this, you are still on Block One and should not move on until you see a successful completion of the end result**. Don't expect perfection, but you should have a sense of your child starting to 'get it.' The biggest indicator of 'getting it' is how **you** feel. You may be tired, yes, but you should feel hopeful. If you are disappointed or even devastated, your child simply needs more time on Block One, and that's fine. **Block One normally takes anywhere from 1-3 days.**

As soon as you get a sense of hope or that a light bulb has lit up in your child's head, it's time to move on to clothes. You don't want to stay in Block One too long. That can result in an 'Only Potty Trained When Naked' kid, and unless you live in a nudist colony, that's not really potty trained. Again, Block One doesn't have to be absolutely perfect. Move on when you have an overall sense of progress.

We are paying more attention to blocks than days here, BUT, but, but...most often the 2nd day of potty training, whatever block of learning you are on, can bring resistance. We will discuss this in the *Drama* and *Dilemmas* chapters more fully, but I want to give you a heads-up early on. By day two, the fun is gone, you are serious about full time potty use, and your child is over it...and cranks up the resistance. Expect it. It's normal and we'll bust through it when it happens.

Block Two

This block still requires your watchful eye. What we are most looking for is to get your child in clothes. Both you and your child should have a sense of when the pee is happening when you start this block. Again, it's not likely going to be in words. Whether with a look or a pee-pee dance, it should look like a light bulb of sorts is going off in your child's head, even if they indicate it by crying or noticing if they don't make it to the potty. That recognition is good!

Commando: Your child should go commando (aka, no underpants but with pants) for about a month, give or take a week. I used to merely suggest this, but over the years I've come to the conclusion that it is a very necessary step. Underpants are too much like a diaper. A few days of potty training is not long enough to reprogram your child's muscle memory. That muscle memory dictates that when something snug goes on, it's time to release the pee and poop. Because this is largely unconscious, it's beyond your child's scope to control it. In other words, she can't be expected to do anything **but** poop and pee in the underpants.

Because they fit snugly, underpants somewhat contain an accident, particularly a poop. While this may seem advantageous, it's not; I've seen kids have accidents in underpants and not be too bothered by it. However, because going commando feels similar to being naked, an accident in pants with no underpants feels much different. To be honest, it feels much grosser. The pee trickles down their legs and their pants get all stuck to them. That's good in potty training. Kids seem to have a sense of shame when an accident happens while going commando that they don't really feel during an accident with underpants. I think this may be because kids see underpants as a diaper in another form. When I say a sense of shame, I'm not suggesting that you shame your child; I don't advocate that. There is, however, a natural sense of shame that develops during the process of socialization, and an internal sense of shame is an indication that socialization is occurring appropriately. Any child can go without underpants under shorts or pants, and on girls, no undies under a dress is perfect.

Another possible reason that kids seem to have more accidents early in potty training if they're wearing undies: underpants afford a certain level of privacy. If the genitals are all tucked away nicely, it seems to the child as though you can't see them having an accident, which reduces the internal sense of shame.

As for cleanliness, going commando is fine hygienically. If you find you have a strong reaction to this suggestion, ask yourself why. I've never seen a kid get an infection or anything like that, which some parents fear. Still, many parents are freaked out by this suggestion. If you are, I'd venture to say you are going to have a hard time potty training. Underpants are a layer of fabric — nothing else.

Pants are a layer of fabric. Going without underpants is not a big deal and can save you lots of frustration. When I hear a parent get wiggly about commando it makes me think they have some weirdness about genitals and pottying, in general. Neither hangup will help in the potty training process. Daycares and commando are another ball of crappy wax entirely. I'll address that in the *Daycare* chapter.

If you're still digging in your heels, go ahead - try underpants if commando totally weirds you out. But if your child starts having accidents left and right? Well, I tole you so.

After a few weeks or so, your child should be able to start using underpants without any problems. If you have tempted your child with fancy character underpants or if your child knows about underpants, you should hide them for now to avoid any fights about it. If your child **begs** for undies, you can give them a go. Some kids have a super high integrity about not peeing on their favorite characters, if you chose character undies. If it works for you, go for it. If not, be willing to ditch them fast.

Also worth noting: you'll be ditching onesies, overalls, footie pajamas, and pants or shorts with complicated buttons and snaps. It seems obvious, but I find it often slips parents' minds. I highly suggest elastic waist bands, at least for a while. Your child is still only going to give you a 5-10 second heads-up, so you need to be quick about getting the pants down. Plus, you want to make it easy for your child to do it herself if she wants to. If your child is hindered by her clothes and can't make it to the potty in time to pee, chances are she will feel really embarrassed and have a meltdown. Set yourself and your child up for nothing but success.

One more note about underpants, commando and the whole shebang: **pull-ups are diapers, plain and simple**. I have no use for them. They prolong potty training indefinitely. No child uses pull-ups as underpants. And if underpants feel too much like a diaper, what do pull-ups feel like? A diaper. Don't waste your time or money.

So, Block Two brings clothes. It also combines with Block Three and brings small outings. These should be planned and will give you a sense of how leaving the house potty trained differs from leaving the house with diapers. Early on, though, these should be small — I repeat, small — outings! Do not attempt a week's grocery shopping. Do not attempt an hour drive to Grandma's. Don't go to story time at the library thinking you'll show off your child's new skill. Do not try to complete a necessary chore. Instead, consider a walk around the block or a run to a store for just one item. These small outings are practice runs.

It is normal for you child to wet a few pairs of pants. The first couple of pees, your child may wet all the way through the pants. Don't be devastated. Have them help you get new clothes and clean up. This is common, but I regularly have moms contacting me who are practically in tears that their child is not getting it. We have no idea how he's processing the information you've given him. Kids do not and cannot just up and do something new because we ask them to. For all we know, he's processing the information and at any moment, he'll discover the right order of things.

You will still be using diapers for naps and bedtime during Block Two. Again, clearly state why the diaper is going on, and when it will come off. You should still be praising or at least acknowledging what your child is learning.

You may find that occasionally, upon prompting your child to use the potty, you will be met with a clear, firm "No." This is different than resistance (which looks more like trying to put a cat in a bucket of water). What I'm talking about here is a simple "No," and when you hear this from your child, you need to respect one of two things:

1. She may not have to go. By the end of these first few days, you should have a handle on her patterns and will pretty much know with at least some warning when she has to pee. I say this because, again, you want to avoid hounding her. You want to have at least a rough idea that

she may have to go, so you're met with success. When a child says clearly that they don't have to go, respect that. A phrase I suggest is, "Okay, I trust you to come tell me when you do. I'll be in the kitchen when you need me." Period. Notice I said 'when,' not 'if,' implying that this **is** going to happen — it's just a matter of time (a subtle shift in language). Don't belabor the point, just tell her where you'll be, which is important because in the beginning phases of training she can't hold it long enough to search for you around the house. Another tactic is to say, "Well, let's try. If nothing comes out, we can try again later." Don't abuse this by trying every 10 minutes. Every half hour or so should yield a pee at some point.

2. Your child is really involved in something at the moment. When you want your child to do something, say it clearly **and give him time to process and respond**. Many parents say, "Come on, it's time to go. I said come here. Now. Let's go. Did you hear me? Come on!" All this in a 20-second time frame. It takes the average toddler 30 seconds to hear, process, and respond. You need only say it once (of course after 30 seconds, your kid could just be digging his heels in and ignoring you). We usually don't like it when our toddlers demand we drop everything that second to attend to them. We ask them to hold on and practice patience. Practice what you preach. Give him the opportunity to finish up what he is doing. Most of the time, he'll come in short order.

In this same category as the second point above is the child who is afraid to miss something while going to the bathroom. This is probably the number one cause of accidents both in the early stages and later. Children get very involved and either forget to think about whether they need the potty, or don't want to miss out. There are a couple of ways to deal with this. You can have the activity come with you: "You can bring your truck with you to the bathroom." Alternately, you can directly address the activity (think in toddler-brain here): "Truck, you wait here. Pascal's going to pee and be right back." Addressing inanimate objects is a great tool for the first month of potty training: "Do you want to show your bear how you pee? Let's bring him to watch." Kids love this. You can set up her favorite dolls in front of the potty to 'teach' them how to do it. Be creative and think like a child. If you're watching a video, have the video 'wait' by pausing it (obviously, much harder to do with a television program).

So, yes, your child may pee and poop through several pairs of pants. For a limited time, this is okay. I have seen it happen a hundred times over. Generally, the child is still processing all the new information. Give them some time to figure things out.

I will make no bones about it. Block Two, which usually comes around 2-6 days from your start date is **the hardest phase**. This is when most people quit potty training. This is when most parents panic. Naked (Block One) goes well, and clothes muck it all up. Keep going. I am not lying. It will click. As they say, "When going through hell...for God's sake, keep going..."

If you find yourself losing patience, take a breather. After all, you're taking a small amount of time to do what the rest of the country is taking a year or longer to do.

Block Two is not only about your child learning. You should be learning as well. Plan not only to learn your child's signals and/or pee-pee dance, but also to learn his pee patterns. Some kids can drink 4 oz of juice and pee seven times in the next hour. Other kids can drink four full sippy cups and hold it for six hours. Seriously. The whole goal here is to find a rhythm to your child's day, and figure out where the potty fits in. If you have a frequent pee-er, you may not want to go anywhere for a while after that first glass of water. On the other hand, if you know you have a camel, go run a couple of errands. Of course, you're not going to know your child's pee habits perfectly after only a few days, but it's the eventual goal.

If there is some minor resistance during Block Two, it's most likely the result of pure toddlerness. There's been a change in routine. Remember that all your child has ever known is a diaper. Since she was a few hours old, she has worn one. She's a little attached. It's okay. This is just something to keep in the back of your mind.

When facing resistance, most parents potty training on their own give up, often by deciding their child is not ready. Nothing could be further from the truth. If your child is capable of fighting for something she wants, she's more than ready for potty training. Resistance can result in a short period of unpleasantness, but then it's done and you're over the hump.

Block Three

This block of learning should be about solidifying the skills. Don't confuse days with blocks. Block Three might start on your second day of potty training. More likely, though, it's going to start somewhere around day 4-10. I'm only mentioning days because I know you need a marker. Seriously, try to let the day thing go. Block Three brings more of the same - watching and prompting. By this time, you can have any combination of things happening. You could have a clear sense of your child 'getting it,' or you could still be lingering somewhere else on the confidence timeline. It's all good. A few days ago, your child had no concept of where pee and poop went. As I discussed in Block Two, resistance could potentially kick up. Alternately, you could be all set to take an eight hour cross-country flight without diapers. The important thing is to stay calm no matter where you find yourself in the process.

There's no better way to help your child hone her potty skills than to take her outside the norm. In this case, that means actually leaving the house for longer than a short walk around the block. For many of you, this is going to coincide with daycare. Daycare, like poop, can be one of the most frustrating aspects of potty training. So, also like poop, I gave it its own glorious chapter.

Leaving home for bigger chunks of time: When heading out for a longer time, be sure you get a good pee before leaving the house. I'm not suggesting bugging your child to pee. Rather, wait to leave till you get that pee, and then hit the road. Again, firm directives work best. "You need to pee before we leave the house, because I will not like it if you pee in the car." If you're pretty sure you have an 11am pooper, don't leave in that time frame (remember this isn't forever — you are still starting out). Bring an extra outfit. I suggest using a cloth diaper or towel to line the car seat. Bring wipes. Hell, bring the potty chair! I'm a huge advocate of bringing the potty chair or insert in the car. It doesn't weigh much and even if your kid poops, you just bring it home. Not much different than carrying around a poopy diaper. You want to plan for accidents. They're going to happen, and it's okay. But chances are, if you keep your small outings small, you may not have any.

One of the most awesome couples I ever worked with took on potty training like a Navy Seal assignment. They had a total tag team plan. The dad took the child out on trials runs all day on the second and third day. Seriously. They went to Target and the market and the library. All just for rest room practice. And you know what? It went really well. I just loved their dedication to getting this down, no matter what the environment. Something to consider.

Blocks Two and Three are by far your hardest chunks of learning. You, the parent, may be feeling insane or incredibly intense. It's normal, but try to chill out. I cannot say this enough: this process can look like a full blown disaster and then clear up. I cannot tell you the amount of mail I get in which a mom goes from being nearly in tears to, "Wow. Never mind, he just sat and peed."

Most often, somewhere during potty training, things are going to seem off. **The following two posts are**

extremely important. Be sure to read them again and again. I'm convinced this is where most parents who try to wing it totally fuck it up. Pay close attention. Seriously, the entire crux of potty training is in these two posts. They address the areas where parents most commonly go wrong: rushing, not prompting, and over-prompting.

Do not overprompt or hover. Almost all resistance is because there is too much 'process' in the process. Certainly, there are some children who are just really difficult to potty train. However, in 95% of the people I've worked with, resistance is the result of hovering parents. Instead of blindly prompting — remember, you are not asking if he has to go — look for signals. Try to find a pattern and a rhythm. If you need to, keep a mental note to not prompt more than once per half-hour. Never, ever, **evah** should the prompting take on a begging, cajoling, negotiating tone. You are not playing *Let's Make A Deal*; you are prompting your child to sit and pee. Period. This can be done firmly without being done meanly.

———————————— *From the Blog* ————————————

PROMPTING

A very common complaint I hear a few days into potty training is something along the lines of, "He's doing fine but only when we tell him to go...is this kid EVER going to tell us when he has to go??"

My answer is: OF COURSE he will!

But right now, in the early stages of potty training, your child needs you. It still counts if they pee in the potty because you tell them to. Like any other learning they have done or will do, they need you — the parent — as a crutch. Think of your child learning to walk. They had to hold your hands at first, both for the physical ability and the comfort. Then they took a few tentative steps away from you but quickly needed your hand again. In strange environments, they hold your hand to tug you along to where they want to investigate. PROMPTING IS HOLDING THEIR HAND.

Some kids will immediately start to self-initiate. Most kids will build it slowly; usually about 3 weeks into the process, you can start counting on self-initiating. Until then, it will be a few days of you always prompting. Then there will be a few days during which they tell you maybe one or two times that they have to go. Then, every once in a while, they will sit on their own and do their business. It will continue to build. And in strange situations, you may have to do some more hand holding. And one day you will wake up and not have potty training on the brain. I swear to god, this day will come.

When to prompt:

The big trick with prompting is to not over-prompt. 90% of all resistance is caused by over-prompting. So the question becomes how often to prompt without slipping into over prompting (aka..bugging, nagging and general over-talking it).

While your child is learning to use the potty, you actually should be learning some things too. I know... WTH, right? What are you supposed to be learning? Your child's pee pattern. Some kids can drink 4 ounces of fluid and pee nine times in an hour. Other kids are camels and can drink 32 ounces of fluid and pee twice all day. Some children are camels until they "break the seal" (college drinking days, anyone?) Then it's nine times in an hour. Every single kid is different. This pee pattern is going to let you get back to regularly-scheduled life after potty training. If you know you have a big drinker and pee-er in the morning, don't go running errands first thing. If you know you have a camel, run like the wind to get your shopping done.

You will also be learning your child's particular pee-pee dance. Some kids have the classic hopping around, ants-in-the-pants dance. Other kids are crotch grabbers. Some kids get real slow and silent. The first few days of potty training should get you acclimated to your child's particular dance. This is naturally a good time to prompt, while simultaneously bringing the child's awareness to the dance. Say something like, "I can see you have to pee. You are holding your penis. Come, sit on the potty."

Remember, you are not asking your child if he has to pee. You are prompting him to use the potty.

There are some other very natural, and therefore low pressure, times to prompt. These are times we all go pee, so the prompts don't have a nagging quality to them and tend not to interrupt the child in the middle of something. These are called easy catches in "elimination communication," or EC (thanks Andrea, of EC Simplified), and they occur: upon awakening and before sleep, before leaving (anywhere) and upon arrival (anywhere), before and after prolonged sitting (high chair, car seat, laps and couches), and before and after an engaging activity.

It's also okay and very natural to hold off on an activity until your child pees, especially when you are very certain they need to. You might say something like, "Sure, we can leave for our walk as soon as you pee," or, "Yes, you can watch Elmo. Sit and pee first." This is not to be confused with bribery or rewarding, which would look something like, "I'll let you watch Elmo if you sit and pee for Mommy." Don't slip into bribery. You will end up with a power struggle.

It's also helpful to prompt as part of a cluster of other things. "Please pick up your blocks. It's time for lunch. Go sit on the potty, then we'll wash hands." This does two things. First, it puts potty training in the normal realm of "Things You Just Do." Second, it keeps your tone and vibe normal. I know this is shocking, but parents can get shrill and anxious around potty training. A brilliant mom on our forum found that talking about using the potty as something 'helpful' worked wonders. Her daughter loves being helpful so she would phrase it as, "Put

*your fork on the table. Put your cup on the table. Go
sit and pee. Thank you. You are such a big help."*

*The delicate dance of prompting without over-
prompting is an important one. It's also important
to remember that this is temporary! Many parents
try to rush the self-initiation and end up with a lot
of accidents. You don't want to do this. If your child
doesn't have a lot of success to build on, his little
mind will go to some version of, "I suck at this. I'm
not even going to try anymore." (I call it the inner
'fuck it'). You are building a tower of success. If you
start kicking out blocks from the foundation, the
tower will tumble.*

OVER-PROMPTING AND BACKING OFF

*It usually goes down like this: a mom writes in
around the 4th or 5th day in of potty training, "I
don't know what happened! It was totally clicking.
She HAD it. She was sitting and peeing and pooping.
Now, all of a sudden, she won't sit on the potty when
I prompt her and she's having accidents all over the
place. HELP!"*

*When you are potty training, there comes a time
when you actually have to hand control over to your
child. Usually, this is within the first week. A really,
really good sign that your child wants you out of*

her business is when she 'had it' and all of a sudden resists or starts have tons of accidents.

The learning phase of anything sucks. No one wants to "be learning"; we like to "have learned."

This is a catch-22, and it's scary as hell. You need to give control over to her, and she's not yet proven she can handle it. Failing to turn over control at the right time is a classic mistake in potty training; because your child isn't self-initiating and going on her own, you figure you have to keep at her.

In reality, what you need to do is give her room to make the right choice for herself. If you are constantly at her — watching, hovering, trying to help,— she has no room to make her potty use her own. Now, this doesn't mean you leave it totally up to her. Prompting is going to be necessary for a bit longer. You must prompt without over prompting, Which sounds awfully Yoda-ish, but it's true.

Here's the trick: toss the prompts out there with as little energy as possible. Something like, "I can see you have to pee. There's your potty." Then drop the matter. Walk away and let it go, mentally and/or physically. Now she can make her own choice, which means there's nothing to resist. If you don't care, there's nothing for her to fight. I mean, of course you care, but you have to give your child the room to learn how to use the potty, choose to do so, and do it herself. The lofty reason for this: it makes the accomplishment her own. The reality: it's easier this way.

Sometimes, you have to take the process out of the process. Here's a direct quote from one of our moms:

"I definitely think the hands-off approach is what we need here. I think experimenting a bit really helped us to figure a few things out. First, we needed to take the potty training out of potty training, if that makes sense at all. I think once we hit a snag Friday we all got too focused on it, and everyone was hyper-aware of every poop/pee/toot that came out of her and we weren't just being a family and spending time together. Tried the complete opposite today. Didn't really talk much about it at all except when I needed to, and kept it short and sweet. I guess the message she is sending me is that she can do it without me and actually does better that way. If I act at all available to help her, she then uses me like a crutch and suddenly can't do anything by herself anymore".

'Zactly.

At the end of Block Three you should have some confidence in being able to leave the house with clothes on (well, at least on your child). You can plan slightly longer outings, maybe to a friend's house. Be mindful though, that you still watch your child for signals. It should already be getting easier to see those signals, but don't get engrossed in a conversation in another room. As I said, bring the potty in the car. I remember bringing it to the beach with Pascal. He actually got out of the water to use his potty! I was impressed that he didn't just pee in the water! I don't think it's necessary to bring the potty into buildings that do have toilets. You don't want to foster any weird attachment to just that one potty (toddlers are notorious for weirdness). I would advise you keep the potty in the back of the car when you're out. You can pee in parking lots, pulled over on the freeway, or whenever you are out and about. I'll address public restrooms later.

You may be laughing — pulled over on the freeway? This is a very important point. If your child indicates that he has to go pee, you drop everything and go! I don't care where you are or what you're doing. GO! You MUST respect your child in this regard. She can not wait a minute, she can not hold on. You've got 5-10 seconds. So yes, if it means pulling over on I-95, that's what you do. Think about it. You've spent all this time and effort and you're finally seeing the pay-off: she's asking you. To risk her not being able to hold it and having an accident would be devastating to her, and I don't use the word devastating lightly. Besides avoiding an accident, you're showing her that you are listening and respecting her needs. This will go a long way toward her doing the same. Don't worry, this is temporary. Your time frame for getting to the potty will keep increasing and very soon, your child will be able to hold her pee and poop until you can get to a regular toilet.

Early in potty training, the pre-pee warning progression will cap off at around 5-10 seconds (meaning that at least for now, when your child signals he has to pee, you have 5-10 seconds to get them to the potty). I have found that they can wait a little longer if you at least respond. Say you're doing dishes in the kitchen and she's in the playroom. If she calls out that she needs to pee, you would say as you're running to her, "I'm coming, please hold it." You will still need to keep an eye on your child at least for another month (although not with the intensity of the first day). Most likely, your child will signal with her pee-pee dance, but if not, you've gotten her pee pattern down and know to prompt her at certain times.

Usually, a few weeks of commando and bringing along the potty is sufficient. After a month, you should be fine. Of course, gauge it for yourself. If you think you need it longer, go for it. Once again, think of how you can support your child in success. You want to line up everything in your and your child's favor!

Blocks Four, Five and Six...to Infinity and Beyond!

By now, you should definitely be seeing quantifiable progress. It will continue to get easier and easier. Rather than keeping notes (for the love of God, please don't keep a pee log!) strive for a rhythm. You want to be in harmony with your child, not hounding him all day long. The parents who do best tend to be very laid back and rely on their intuition. There's really no rule book here, just learning.

You will keep building on success. I often refer to this as "stacking successes." You want to pay close attention to your child's successes, and not harp on the failures. If your child is making it to the potty more than not, it's good. If she has five pees on the pot and two misses, that's good. Yes, it needs improvement, but it's good. It's human nature to pick out the bad. I used to own a children's clothing store. Almost all of my customers were awesome, but still, I would go home bitching about the one customer who blew my day. We all do this, but try to step out of it while potty training. Yes, we want to fix problems, but we don't want to come down on the child all the time.

These may very well maybe the weirdest, hardest few days of your parenting career. It can be tedious, doing this dance of balancing vigilance with casualness. It will feel like it's taking a lot longer than it is. In the grand scheme, you're potty training in a short period of time. I cringe when I see people taking a year to potty train. They will encounter the same struggles you will, only theirs will be super-prolonged.

Should things seem like they're progressing, but at a slower rate than you anticipated, that's okay. Continue at a slower rate. If there appears to be a major snafu and you're seeing **no** progress, check out specific solutions in the *Drama* and *Dilemmas* chapters. Potty training isn't rocket science, but it isn't a single simple scenario, either. Every child is different and I think I've seen every possible situation. I will say that almost all problems can be solved by relieving any kind of pressure, whether it be pressure to maintain a social calendar, to prove yourself, to do this right, or to potty train in exactly three days or fewer.

Most people don't have any trouble at all. Most likely, your child's signals will be pretty clear to both of you. You will probably feel a new bond with this Big Kid. You are going to be amazed at your kid's self-pride. You are going to be blown away by what she is capable of. Seriously...this is going to rock your world. One of the absolute coolest things I've found about potty training is it gives you a look into your child's psyche. You gain insight into your child's learning methods and curve, and that's wonderful!

Not every kid learns the same way. Good teachers know this. When a student isn't learning, they find a back door to teaching, and they get creative. So many parents give potty training a whirl — a half-assed whirl, usually — and are quick to throw a diaper back on because they 'aren't getting it.' Man. There would be like three kids left in school if teachers threw in the towel when students 'didn't get it.' When your child isn't learning something, you amp up the teaching, no? You don't ditch it.

We have no way to know how your child will learn this until you jump in. It's important to remember that this is probably the first thing you are actively teaching and the first thing he is actively learning. That is to say, this is the first case in which you're teaching and he's learning something that must take place in a certain order, and for which there really is only one "right" outcome. The more you can look at potty training as just something you are teaching your child, the better off you are going to be.

Underpants, self-initiation and night/nap dryness all sort of blend into the recipe at around three weeks after your start date. Use your parental intuition and judgement; I know you have it! Push the limits a little. Don't be fearful. Remember, above all, your vibe and energy are running the show.

To recap, progressing through the blocks of learning is what's important. Don't track this by days. Make sure to meet the goals of each block before moving on. The transition points from pre-potty training to Block One, and from Block One to Block Two, are where most parents panic. It's okay. Move through those transitions. You are looking for progress, not perfection. You are looking for forward movement. If your child races to the potty but has an accident on the way, that's awesome; he was moving in the right direction. Evaluate success through the lens of a teacher who is looking for progress.

And have wine handy. Or really good chocolate.

Chapter 6: Night Time Training

Before we launch into night time training, let me state something very clearly: I have separated out nighttime from daytime because to potty train for both at once looks very overwhelming to most parents, particularly those who work full time out of the home. **But potty training for night and day at the same time is the most effective way to potty train.** It will be more chaotic for a few days, but in the long run you will have almost zero hassles down the road. When there is no back up — no other option — there are no power struggles (what's there to fight for?) There's less confusion and less withholding of pee and poop. When you make using the potty the new way of doing things day AND night, it becomes second nature much faster. It's totally up to you, and I won't judge either way, but I just have to throw it out there that tackling day and night at the same time is the better way to train. To do both at the same time, you would simply follow the daytime instructions as I described them in the previous chapter, adding in the nighttime instructions addressed here. Give this some serious thought before you make a decision one way or another.

The biggest thing to remember about nighttime is that it's a long-ass time. That's the major difference between naps and night. Toddlers should be sleeping anywhere from 9-13 hours each night; that's a long time to go without peeing! Think about it; most adults wake up to pee at least once a night and we're **skilled** at using the potty.

I've searched and searched for the Magic Night Time Trick; it doesn't exist. There's no way around it. To train for nighttime, you have to:

1) carefully monitor fluid intake before bedtime and/or
2) wake your child to pee.

Sorry. I wish there were a magic trick I could give you. I do, however, have some tips to make night training a lot easier on you.

You will want to monitor fluids about 2-3 hours before bedtime, making sure there's minimal intake. This can be hard on your child if you do it suddenly. If your kid is used to lots of fluid before bed, I would start by scaling back gradually before you attempt your first diaperless night. Avoid sippy cups and bottles at night (really, these shouldn't be used at nighttime now anyway). The sucking action leads kids to take in more than they would if they were using a cup. A great trick I've learned is to buy tiny cups: sake cups, mini-tea cups or even shot glasses. This gives the illusion of a full glass, even though there's very little liquid in it. Also, kids love little things that are their size. I know quite a few moms who've developed a lovely night time tea ritual with their kids (chamomile tea is widely accepted as promoting sleep and calm). Little cups also come in handy for the classic bedtime stall, "I need a drink of water." If your kid pulls this, you can use a tiny cup to give him a drink without worrying he's taking in too much fluid.

How do you plan for a reduction in fluids before bed? Think of the day in terms of two upside down pyramids. One pyramid spans the time from waking to nap, the other spans the time from nap waking to sleep. The width of the pyramid represents the amount of fluid your child should be drinking; go heavy on fluids upon awakening, and then taper to almost nothing about an hour before nap and at least two hours before bedtime. If your child is used to having a big glass of something with dinner, this habit needs to change. Making the change can be tricky for a day or so, but your child will get used to it. You'll then need to withhold fluids from dinner on. Withholding fluids before sleep will naturally make your child thirstier in the morning, which works perfectly with the fluid pyramid. Most kids have drinking patterns that resemble right-side up pyramids. The child is used to a decent-sized drink before bed. If your kid falls into this category, start the fluid-tapering song-and-dance before you actually intend to begin night training. After all, you know toddlers and change — not good.

If you are still nursing intermittently throughout the night, night training could be a little trickier. Generally speaking, however, most kids at this age are nursing for comfort rather than volume, so they may not be taking in much fluid. Also, you could have your child pee before or after nursing. Pick whichever option best fits your child. Some kids like to pee before nursing, most prefer it afterward. Either is fine, but the trick is consistency.

If you are co-sleeping, the good news is that night training is much easier. Your child has no travel time, and usually gets restless right before needing to pee, which will help alert you to the situation. It's also a lot easier on you if all you need to do is roll over as opposed to walking down the hall to your child's room. That said, though, if you haven't ever had the desire to co-sleep, I wouldn't recommend starting just to make night training easier.

As for waking up your child to pee, I recommend starting with two wakings, so you can establish in your own mind when during the night your child does her peeing. Does she pee at 10pm and 2am? At 12am and 4am? Some kids pee an hour after going down, some kids pee once at 3am. If you do two wakings for a week or so — I recommend 10pm and 2am wakings at first, though you can adjust as needed — you should begin to develop a good idea of when your child is peeing. Unfortunately, unless you want to stay up all night, there's a bit of guess work here, which is why if you find your child isn't peeing at 10pm or 2am, you may want to adjust the waking times. Even if your child's diapers have been dry upon waking in the morning lately, you might want to try at least one waking for a short time at the beginning of night training. The idea behind this is not just to catch the pee, but also to train your child's body to wake up if he needs to go. Unfortunately, the idea of waking to pee isn't something you can explain to the child in words. It has to be learned physically, through waking. (Sorry!)

Here's the easiest, least disruptive way to go about handling these wakings. Set your cell phone alarm so you don't have the blaring alarm clock going off in the middle of the night. Have the potty chair right next to the child's bed. It's best if she wears two-piece pajamas for the sake of simplicity, especially in the winter. Don't wake your child too soon after she's gone to sleep, or too soon before you expect her to wake up for morning. This would result in her waking fully, which is something nobody wants! Unless your child wakes fully at the drop of a pin, I wouldn't worry about her waking for good if you rouse her to pee in the middle of the night. She's likely to stay at least partially asleep. The harder part is holding up her limp weight. Mostly-asleep kids are kind of like wet spaghetti. Heavy, wet spaghetti. Get her to the potty, and then you can just hold her up and whisper for her to pee. I've always found it helpful to make a sshhhing noise (similar to the sound of peeing) in the child's ear. Even half asleep, your child may indicate she don't have to pee. Just pull up her pajamas and put her back down. A really good trick is to use a big plastic party cup (or any similarly-sized reusable container). You can just stand your child up — this works for both girls and boys — and have her pee in it. Mostly-asleep kids are easier to hold this way, since they're taking some of their own weight, and the whole thing goes quickly and smoothly.

It seems obvious to me but I'll say it anyway: you don't want to turn on bright lights and try to lug your child to the bathroom (hence the suggestion that you keep the potty near your child's bed). If you do, you'll have yourself a wide-awake toddler party at 2am. Not desirable.

Once you figure out approximately when your child is typically peeing at night, you can cut down to just one waking. I have found that it helps a lot to tell your child — right before he goes to sleep — to hold his pee until you come for him. It's his last conscious thought this way, and works its way into his subconscious. You can then start scooching the time of the pee waking a little bit each night, till it's about two hours before his normal morning wake up time. If he can make it to 2 hours before his normal wake up, that's a good sign that he can hold it all night.

Eventually, your child will either be able to hold it all night or will wake up to ask to pee. You'll know she's ready to go all night when she routinely say no or shakes her head during the wake-up pee. Even if it starts to look like she's able to hold it all night, continue to monitor fluids in the evening. If she shows the ability to wake up (by herself) to pee, you don't have to be so vigilant. Either scenario is equally acceptable.

Nighttime potty training can take longer than daytime potty training, but won't necessarily. Each child is different and each parent's level of commitment is different. Be gentle with yourself and realistic with your capabilities. As with day training, repetition and consistency are the most important factors. If you absolutely know you are unable to wake up to assist your child, then you may need to be an ultra-vigilant fluid monitor before bed. The reverse is also true: if you simply cannot monitor fluids before bed, commit to waking up. You do need to deal with night training at some point.

IS NIGHT TRAINING NECESSARY?

Yes. Or maybe no. How's that for a solid answer?

Many, many children will start staying dry on their own as they get better and better at holding and consolidating during the day. A really good indicator that a child is ready for night training is when they start staying dry for their nap. HOWEVER, THIS ISN'T TRUE FOR EVERY KID. So, don't wait for that necessarily but should your child start staying dry during naps, go for it!

On that note, there is no such thing as JUST nap training. You can always try to go with a diaper for nap but there is NOTHING we can do to assist the child (ie, you can't wake a child mid-nap to help them empty their bladder).

It's always best to ditch all diapers as soon as you are able. But night training can be wonky because there REALLY is an issue of whether or not the child's bladder is able to hold and consolidate for such a long time.

My bottom line is that night training can be on the back burner until around 3-3 and a half. If it hasn't naturally occurred by then, YOU MUST ATTEND TO IT. The bladder is being developed at this age and if it develops fully without the practice of holding and consolidating, those muscles will atrophy and you will struggle indefinitely with bedwetting.

I can, in no way know for certain what is true for every single child out there. I just can't. But I can see trends in the thousands of kids I have worked with. A very real and serious trend I see is that once a child is past the age of 4, night training becomes near impossible.

I regularly get clients, including pediatricians with 5, 6, and 7 year olds in night time diapers (pull-ups, which are diapers). They think they don't have to attend to night training and time just keeps marching on. And then the child's muscles are atrophied and night training is incredibly hard.

Now granted, there are some truly tough and rare cases. But the sheer volume of kids currently over 4 in night diapers is not right. It's not an issue of the kids not being able to do it. It's an issue of the wicking of disposables, the child not feeling the wetness, and aggressive marketing on the part of the big diaper companies.

So, no. You don't have to dive into night training if you don't feel up to it yourself. Or if your child has been struggling with sleep. Or if you're struggling with sleep. But I can't say it enough. Do not go past 3 and a half without attending to it.

Completely random side note to end this chapter. If you are over 32 weeks pregnant with another child, it's so totally cool to put off night training until the baby is around 4-6 weeks. You need to rest, save energy for labor and birth, and adjust to life with a newborn. You can attend to night training when you are waking for night feedings for the baby. There is no reason to stress yourself out with night training right now. Unless, of course, you want to. Then go for it, Mama.

Nighttime Accidents

Nighttime accidents are inevitable. Some nights your child might drink too much fluid, and others, you might simply forget to wake (or sleep through waking) your child. As these accidents are inevitable, I've found a pretty good way to deal with them: while your child is going through the transition from diapers to diaperless at night, keep an extra pair of pajamas and a thick fleece blanket near the bed. Should your child have an accident, change her pajamas and be sure to ask or sit her on the potty in case she has more pee — often she won't have emptied her bladder completely. Instead of changing sheets in the middle of the night, simply place the fleece blanket over the wet sheet. The fleece will keep the pee from soaking her dry pajamas. This may sound gross to some, but it sure beats having to change the sheets when you're both half-awake. Of course, change the sheets in the morning. One more thing: night time accidents are all on you. The capability to hold the pee until morning or to be able to wake herself up to pee develops over time, and if your child can't do it yet, she can't do it yet — you have to wake her to pee until her body is ready to consolidate and hold through the night.

If your child is consistently (as in, every night) having nighttime accidents, adjust something. You don't have to abandon night training. You may, however, need to change the times you wake him or monitor his fluids even more closely. Be creative and do what works for you and your family.

If night training looks like a full-blown disaster after a week of attempts — I mean, you are barely sleeping and are still missing the pees — your child might be an extremely deep sleeper. CAVEAT: this is not common. If you suspect your child is a really deep sleeper, you might look into one of the few different alarm products on the market. These alarms wake your child just as she is beginning to pee. Personally, I have never used any of these, but I've heard excellent reports from the parents who have.

Chapter 7: Block One Drama

In this chapter, I will address the common problems in the first week of potty training. If you are having difficulties, read through all the drama chapters. Problems can crop up at any point in potty training, not just during Block One. Separating problems by block is just my attempt to keep an overwhelming amount of information semi-organized.

Okay. So you are making your way through Block One of potty training. I'm sure you are exhausted. It's very odd how exhausting watching your child is, huh?

You are most likely reading this chapter because you are unsure of how things are going. Or you know for a fact things are not going well. You may have a great feeling, or you may be devastated. Or confused. Or unsure. Yes, you will run the gamut of emotions for the next week, I'm sure. Regardless of how you're feeling about potty training, do not let a successful (or failed) poop or pee in the potty determine your emotional state. In fact, it's a good idea never to let your toddler's behavior dictate your emotional state, though I know that's easier said than done. Remember, though, potty training progress is not a measurement of your parenting abilities, nor of how smart your child is.

Having said that, let's go through and see where you're at and what, if anything, you need to do differently. Remember the time line of potty training: **Clueless** to **I peed** to **I'm peeing** to **I have to pee**. We are looking for progress, not perfection! I'm going to refer alternately to "blocks" and "days," because no matter how much I want you to avoid tracking progress by days, you are going to.

There are really, honestly, truly no disasters in the first couple of days of potty training. There can't be; it's too new. You are changing a routine, a habit that has been in place for somewhere around two years. That's not going to happen in a day.

No poop: The most common cause for a parental freak-out is not getting a poop on the first day. You may have noticed that poop has its very own chapter. Yeah. It's that big a freaking deal. Do not worry if there's no poop on the first day. Your child was most likely a once-, twice-, or three-times-a-day pooper when she was diapered. Almost every child I've ever worked with goes down to one poop a day during potty training. I think this consolidation of poops is natural. Most adults only poop once a day, if that. There's nothing to worry about from a medical standpoint if your kid has a day or two of no pooping. For many kids, that first day of potty training is very strange - all this focus on a previously unnoticed thing - and there's bound to be some performance anxiety.

If there's no poop, don't sweat it. Carry on like normal. Be aware, though, that a poop is most certainly coming at some point. Go look over the *Poop* chapter and see if anything there pops out at you. But honestly, especially on the first day, this is normal.

A crazy amount of pee: If your child seemed to spend the whole day peeing and not noticing, you most likely overdid the fluid consumption. Just go back to a normal amount of liquid. Remember, kids under 24 months in particular can't seem to handle excessive fluid intake. On the flip side, do make sure you're monitoring fluid intake to some degree. This doesn't mean you should restrict liquids, it just means keep an eye out for when and how much your child drinks relative to when and how much he pees so you can get a handle on his normal patterns.

Hardly any pee at all: So, you gave your child five extra juices boxes, which would normally yield eight diaper changes. With the diapers off, however, your child has suddenly become a camel. If you only got a few pees on day one, it's okay. Some children can really hold it. You don't have to assume she is purposely withholding the pee, just that she can control her bladder. That's awesome. A child who can hold it is preferable to one who has to go every time there's even a small amount of pee in her bladder. Don't necessarily increase the fluid intake, but rather try to get a handle on her pee patterns. Start to get a feel for how long she can hold it after taking in fluid so you can predict the most appropriate times to prompt. My best friend's husband pees once a day — I kid you not. Also, the dude has never had a urinary tract infection. Some people are just camels. However, beware the camel...once the "seal" is broken, so to speak, many camels pee several times in a short period.

Absolutely no awareness of having peed: Ok, you're chill with the notion of progress rather than perfection, you're relaxed that your kid isn't going to figure this all out in a day, you are not freaking out...but geez Louise, this kid is showing **no** recognition that he just peed. WTH?

This happens most often in children under 22 months. Regardless of your child's age, however, you'll want to make sure she truly is 'clueless,' rather than simply ignoring the pee. 'Clueless' means...clueless. How's that for a rock solid definition? The child who pees and pretends it didn't happen is NOT clueless. See the difference? The truly clueless will pee while walking, slip on it, fall, and have no idea what the hell just happened. If, by the end of day one, your child is still totally clueless, it's okay. All it means is that you are still in Block One. If your child pees and pretends it doesn't happen, however...

Kid pees and pretends it doesn't happen: For this kid, remind him that pee goes in the potty. Frown or make an otherwise displeased facial expression and say, "No pee on the floor. Pee goes in the potty." Make those statements in that specific order, putting the **desired result** last. Kids tend to remember the last thing you said a little better; it just seems to stick. You don't want to be mean or reprimanding, but you do need to express that peeing on the floor is NOT good and peeing in the potty IS good.

As for handling the accident, don't panic. You want to have him help you clean up and sit on the potty to finish eliminating any pee he may have left. You can say something to the effect of ,"I know you are learning, AND your pee goes in the potty." **Do not** say, "It's okay." I'll repeat this a lot. This phrase seems to imply permission (to pee on the floor) to some kids, even if what you really mean to express is, "My head is not going to explode or anything." Essentially, acknowledge that he's still learning while consistently reinforcing the idea that pee goes in the potty.

The two seconds you turned your back...: You've hardly been breathing, watching like a hawk for her pee-pee dance, a sign, a twitch, a signal. Nada. So you have to pee or get more coffee (or beer) and the **two freaking seconds** your back is turned, she pees right there on the floor. Argh. How is this possible? Well, there's good news: this kid is well on her way to being potty trained. If she can hold it until the two seconds you turn your back, yep, that kid is almost done potty training. Think about it. Most likely, this is her way of asking for privacy. Remember, even though we don't think of it this way, a diaper conceals bodily functions, so it provides some privacy, right? Even though we see and clean up the messy diaper afterward, she still had privacy during the act of eliminating. Now her bum's in the breeze and there's no privacy. It's very cool to want privacy. It's the natural progression of potty training. So give her some. When you think it's about time for her to go, set her up on the potty and conveniently "forget" something in the other room. If she's using an insert on the big potty, it's the same deal, and you can close the bathroom door partially. Nine times out of ten, she'll pee the second you leave the room. This goes for poop too.

Also, whenever you have to pee during the beginning phases of potty training, bring your child with you. This is a great thing to do together. It normalizes and models the behavior. It's an all-around win.

The kid who does absolutely no signalling whatsoevah: Okay. Again, you're watching like a hawk and for the life of you, you can NOT see any sort of signal. Now, I don't want to seem contrary, but every single child has a signal. I'm not saying you weren't watching for it; I know you were. It's just that for some kids, the signal is really subtle. A former client was convinced her daughter, Jessie, had no signal. On the second day of potty training — Jessie was still naked at this point — she finally saw it: Jessie crossed her big toe over the middle toe when she needed to pee. WEIRD, right? Subtle, and small, and not in the general "potty area" of the body. This is part of the reason I insist on at least one naked day. Every kid has some sort of pause or signal right before they pee. I'm not saying it's going to be big or obvious, but if you look closely, you'll see something. The pre-pee signal could be a pause in speech, a look he gets in his eye, a twitch in his jaw, or any number of other possibilities. If you really can't see it, try to look at your kid through squinty eyes, if that makes sense. You know those optical illusion posters where you have to find the fish in the psychedelic colors, and the only way to find the fish is to squint? Yeah, it's kind of like that. So many parents get focused on the genitals — makes sense, since that's where the eagle is landing — or they have an expectation of what the signal is going to be. Let the preconceived notions go. Just watch with squinty eyes. And above all, keep your child's pee pattern in mind. If you know approximately when the pee should be coming, it makes it easier to watch for the signal.

Sir Dribbles-A-Lot: This kid is a dripping faucet. I mostly see dribblers in boys, which kind of figures, yeah? They can dribble a lot throughout the day, or it might occur right before they have to pee. This is not terribly worrisome in the first few days. You have to remember that yesterday, when and how to pee wasn't on his radar. Today he's getting used to a whole new ballgame. We don't know for sure how your child peed when he was wearing a diaper. He might have let the pee out a little at a time until the diaper was full. For this kid, part of potty training is a natural consolidation of those little dribbly pees into one bigger one. It generally happens naturally as they get the hang of things.

The kid will not sit long enough to pee: This is a very common complaint. Try doing something to engage her and keep her attention while she's on the potty. I offer suggestions like singing a song, counting to a particular number together (50 is a good one), or reading some books. A great phrase to use is: "I need to **hear** more pee." For some reason, this resonates with kids better than, "sit and finish your pee." I think it's because the kids are motivated to give you something other than the actual pee. They want to give you the **sound** of pee. What. Ever. Toddlers.

But this particular issue is also one of the places in which parenting philosophies can kind of muck things up. Your child is getting to an age of limit-testing. You need to be able to be firm and let your child know you mean business. For some parents, though, "being firm" feels sticky. Let me tell you that it's okay to be firm. You don't need to be mean to be firm. The less "dancing around" your child you do, the better. Sometimes, parents go so over the top trying to get the child to sit and pee that it turns into serious entertainment for the kid. You don't want to set that habit up. Also, if you're bending over backward to get the kid to pee, it starts to smell like fear. Kids can smell fear a mile away, and it will either make **them** fearful or they will eat you for breakfast.

So what can you do? Some mild form of distraction is fine. I would stay away from TV, though. Don't put the potty in front of a video or program and let your child just sit there. It may get them to sit but it is way too passive. They are just getting the pee in the potty by chance because they happen to be sitting there. What they need to be learning is to act on the feeling of having to pee.

On that note, phone games, tablets, and other electronic devices as potty entertainment are okay for the first couple of days **if you have to**. I don't suggest them ,but some parents specifically ask. Just don't make it a habit. As with TV, these devices make the peeing/pooping passive, and can quickly lead to manipulation (the child demands a reward in order to pee or poop). My bottom line is that if your child can play a game on a mobile device, your child is more than capable of putting pee and poop in the potty.

Remember, the idea is to normalize the use of the potty, not to make it into a big game or special thing.

The "Calm Jar": This is a distraction that works well for a few different situations. Make a "Calm Jar" out of a mason jar or a clear plastic water bottle. Fill it with water, medium-sized glitter, and some oil or glycerin. The result is a sort of snow globe. Many parents use the "Calm Jar" in lieu of a time out: the child can shake it and watch the glitter settle, which is calming and relaxing and takes a minute. I've found the "Calm Jar" to be excellent for kids who want to pop right up off the potty because it helps keep their interest, which keeps them seated. It's also great for the kid who's having trouble releasing pee or poop. This is the kid who sits on the n't seem to let the pee go; then she pops up and floor. This kid is not screwing with you, even oks like it— she just needs to sit longer and allow ase. The "Calm Jar" will help her relax and let the owing.

Fear of the potty: You've been casual and relaxed. You know you are not putting any pressure on your child. Still, your kid seems afraid of the potty. First of all, do **not** invalidate her feelings. Just like fear of the dark, the monster under the bed, or the vacuum, this is a real fear (however illogical it might be). We don't want to feed into it, but we don't want to invalidate it. Never ask your child if she is afraid of the potty. You will get a "yes," and there's nowhere to go from there. Instead, tell her something along the lines of, "Honey, I know this can feel weird. I know it's brand new. Look at the potty. See? It's just plastic." Let her practice pouring some water into it and dumping it into the big toilet. Practice with some toys or dolls, having her "help" them use the potty. I've even had moms sit right on the darn thing and pee to show it's not gonna bite (very bendy moms, I should add). You can even have her sit on it (when she doesn't need to go pee) for practice. Again, don't feed into the fear, but do acknowledge it. Acknowledgment goes a long way with kids. This is one of those times to use an "and" sentence construct: "Yes, I know it feels strange **and** that's where your pee goes." Yes and yes.

Also, check out my musings on this subject in the *Poop* chapter. There are many things that contribute to potty fear. You have to work through this fear, and it may take a fair amount of creativity. Just as fearing a monster under the bed doesn't mean you don't go to bed, fear of the potty doesn't mean you put a diaper back on. Also, try to pin down the fear. Is she afraid of the potty itself, or the sensation of pooping? It helps to know what's worrying her so you can deal with it more specifically.

Also, you'll want to identify whether you're looking at a case of true fear or just a little bit of resistance. The child with a true, deep fear of the potty is rare and should be distinguished from a child who is showing resistance. In the case of a child with a true fear, the potty might as well be filled with boiling, molten lava — she wants no part of it. The truly afraid child is the one who, right from the get go, shrieked and hollered and had to be dragged to the potty. Note that a true fear shows up right from the start of potty training. A child who starts resisting after using the potty a couple of times isn't truly AFRAID. Many children show resistance to the potty. Fear is something different. You will recognize it if you see it, but you're not likely to. In all my years, of all the kids I've worked with, only eleven have fallen into this category. I hesitate even to mention it because I don't want everyone saying, "This is my kid." I'll talk more about the truly fearful child in *Special Circumstances*.

So, are you sensing a theme here? In case you're too exhausted to put it together, I'll spell it out. **Nothing** is "wrong" the first day of potty training. Yesterday, your kid could pee and poop whenever, wherever the urge struck. Now, you are on him like white on rice and he is expected to up and make this huge change. Just remember that.

Also, never underestimate the power of sleep. Much will be accomplished in his sleep tonight. Information gets sorted out in the brain and you can begin fresh in the morning.

If you feel that Block One went pretty well — that there was some forward movement and some clicking — rock on. That's awesome. Move on to Block Two: pants, commando, and small outings. If you are feeling less-than-stellar or simply a little unsure, it's okay to bounce a little from Block One to Block Two. I recommend having your child go half naked and half clothed. I call it...

Handing your child success: Often, parents are just not really sure where their kid is at with regard to taking everything in during the early phases of potty training. If you fall into this category, it's okay to do more naked time. To make progress, though, we need to start stacking up successes. This will build your child's pride and confidence. Learning to use the potty is a lot like learning to read. You can't just learn a letter and move on. You have to study the letter, hear it again and again, and write it in lower and upper case many, many times (I have a small rain forest in worksheets that prove this). To create progress in potty training, you have to nudge the child forward with the expectation that they can rise to the next challenge, but you also have to know they've gotten the last step. It's a balancing act, to be sure.

One way to hand your child success in Block Two is to start with your child naked (at least from the waist down) and make sure you get a good pee in the potty. Then throw on some clothes for a very small outing. Bracket the day's activities around pees, trying to ensure that you're home and your child has a naked bum for the times when he needs to go. Between pees, do small errands or activities outside. Many parents feel like this is cheating, but it's not. Or it is, and I don't care. The most valuable outcome here is that your child will feel pride and accomplishment. **These will provide the ongoing motivation**.

Between Block One and Block Two, parents often try to rush things a bit. Get pants on the kid. Get out of the house. Get the kid fully potty trained. Part of the reason for clearing your social calendar is to be able to be able to have an, "Eh, whatever," attitude about the whole thing. If you rush things, you'll be kicking out those blocks of success! They are vital. Without them, your tower is going to be very unstable, if it stands at all. Take your time, and set your child up to succeed.

Another thing: be sure **you** are taking care of yourself. Yes, this can be tiring. Yes, have some wine. But do not stay up late or eat a ton of junk. We need you sane and rested so you can be the most effective teacher possible, yeah?

Chapter 8: Block Two and Three Dilemmas

At this point, you should feel pretty comfortable that your child, while bare bummed, can sit and pee on the potty. Remember: it's okay if you are still prompting. Prompting counts as success and your child needs it. Remember, though; don't over-prompt (she says to the mom holding a knife). By now, you may have started with pants, or your child may still be butt nekkid, or you may be doing a mix of the two.

Resistance!!! (whoo-hoo!): This phase of potty training can bring about resistance. Regardless of what block you are on, resistance usually hits on the second day of potty training. Your kid is thinking, "This was okay when we started. But now...oh no, you might possibly be serious about this peeing-in-the-potty thing." The second day of potty training is most commonly the day when parents without a plan (ahem, this book) give up. They think the resistance is a sign that the child is not ready. In reality, nothing could be further from the truth. If your child is able to put up a fight for something he wants, he's more than ready to put his pee in the potty.

I simply cannot tell you how many times I hear some version of what former client Aislinn wrote: "I can't believe it! This looked like SUCH a disaster. I swear I was ready to give up. Thank god I didn't! Working through that resistance was not fun but now it's the fourth day and she's GOT IT! Yahoo!"

The biggest reason for resistance is that you're "on it" too hard with your kid. You probably don't even realize how much pressure you're putting on your child, but most parents go through this at some point. You can't help it. You have potty on the brain, and you are on edge. If your kid is resisting, you are most likely over-prompting.

Remember those two posts you read about prompting and backing off? The ones I said were really important? The ones you probably read way back two weeks ago, when you were thinking about potty training in theory but weren't actually doing it yet? Yeah. Read them again, now that you're in the thick of it. I'm not kidding when I say most problems can be solved with the information contained in those two posts. They'll help you strike the balance between over-prompting and backing off.

For some children, everything "clicks" during the first few days of potty training, but for a good majority it doesn't. Before we get to actual dilemmas, we need to review a few things. First, remember that all this was absolutely not on your child's radar a couple of days ago. I know I keep saying that, but it's important for you to really hear it. We have to allow them time to learn this. Most parents realize this on some level, but still have a sort of lingering hope that everything will be signed, sealed and delivered on the second or third day. As with any major milestone, mastering the potty takes time, and having a "potty prodigy" is highly unlikely. It can happen, yes. But I don't want you to feel weird or like you're doing a crappy job if it doesn't.

Side note for a second: I really believe potty training pains are like labor pains. I think they get fuzzy around the edges with time. Most of the people who say their kid upped and decided not to wear diapers on his own have a kid older than yours. Or they're new in town. For whatever reason, you can't really verify their story. I hear about the "potty prodigy" all the time from moms on the playground. In reality, though, I hang around with a lot of moms and potty training is my job, and I've yet to see with my own eyes the kid who just potty trains himself in hours. Just want you to know that so your head doesn't blow off.

Another important thing to remember is that every child has her own learning methods and curve. It's okay if she doesn't take to potty training as fast as you expected. It doesn't mean your child is not smart.

Having said that, here are some very common problems in Block Two of potty training.

Peeing right through the pants: Your kid did **great** with Block One. **Great.** You knew she was ready to move on. Got her up, took off the diaper, she peed first thing, you put her in some pants and she's peeing right the hell through them all. It's 11:30am and you have 7 pairs of soaking pants. WTF, Jamie?

Okay. Number one: does she actually know how to manipulate her clothing? This is a very big issue, and yet we all tend to forget about it. I discussed it in Chapter 4 but again, you probably glossed over it because it didn't seem very important two weeks ago when you first read the book. It's important. If she has to pee and has trouble getting her pants down, she will lose a few vital seconds. You want her to practice actually pushing her pants down when she DOESN'T need to use the potty so the skill is in place when she does.

Be sure she's in very loose, elastic waist pants or shorts or leggings. For girls, dresses with no panties work great. For boys, boxers are pretty magical, but make sure he is commando. This means he's wearing boxers and only boxers, not boxers as undies. The idea behind this is that they need as little fabric on the bum as possible. Again, I know we talked about this already, but it's worth repeating.

The feeling of having to go pee: Start using the phrase, "The feeling of having to go pee..." with your child. Some kids don't realize they need first to **feel it,** then make the move to the potty, then take the pants down, then sit and pee. Most kids respond best to short, direct commands. You don't have to bark this out like you're training a dog, but be short and direct, and state things **in the order you would like them done.** This is vital. Potty training is the first thing your child is learning that has a set order with only one desirable outcome. That order can get mixed up, so make sure your kid is clear: Go. Pants. Sit. Pee.

Many kids hear you say, "Go pee!" and they do. It always reminds me of that old movie *Parenthood,* with Steve Martin. His daughter feels sick and he says, "Honey, do you feel like you have to throw up?" And she says, "Okay" and pukes all over him. Yeaaah. You want specific, short directions to indicate what they should be doing.

Let's look at other versions of the peeing through pants. Sometimes, it's just that your child hasn't nailed that first block of learning. He should be able to pee on the potty when prompted or on his own naked. If he can't/won't do that, you should hold off the pants. Don't try to rush pants and don't think of wearing pants as a marker of success. It's simply the next block of learning. We can't stack the "pants block" until we get the "naked block" down. Now you don't, of course, want a potty-trained-when-naked kid, so you will need to nudge the process along. If you are unsure of what to do, try pants. If the pants get wet, 'hand your child success,' as I discussed at the end of the last chapter.

If you think your child is trying to get to the potty, but just isn't making it, keep going. Trying but not making it in time is a really good sign! If she is wetting through a few pairs of pants but you still feel pretty hopeful, keep going. I've had so many parents say what former client Amy said:

On the Forum

"I just wanted to offer hope to those who may be feeling unsuccessful. The first couple of days resulted in many accidents. My daughter Katherine (22 months) would start to pee on the floor, stop when I told her to hold it, not pee on the pot, and then have an accident right afterwards. Day two resulted in nine pairs of pants in seven hrs (and two bare-bottomed accidents, as Kat liked being naked).

The thing that helped me the most after the first couple of days was reading your blog entry about how parents have to be committed to this and not think that she wasn't ready yet and to wait a few more months. This morning I had a renewed resolve that this was it. I reminded Kat that she's a big girl now and doesn't use diapers anymore (except for sleeping, but I didn't remind her of that). She's acting like a big girl at mealtimes, too, not wanting to wear a bib and wanting to use grown up utensils & plates! This has only been since potty training . She's been nursing more often today, but I think all the big girl responsibility is getting to her. I have to remind myself not to call her my baby.

I just wanted to say thank you, Jamie! And I'm so glad I stuck it out!"

Wet pants can be part of the learning process. Overall, if the child is not getting pee in the potty, what you should be looking for are signs of:

Distaste — they should feel yucky and it should register.
Apologeticness — any version of sorry
Dismay — they are bothered that this happened
Hiding — they are trying to hide it from you (this can also be flat out denial that they peed their pants)

Any of those signs show that your child is aware of and has negative feelings about peeing her pants. This is when you would use the half naked/half clothed technique. She probably needs a tiny bit more learning and a bit more confidence in her own abilities.

If your child pees her pants and registers nothing at all, it's definitely time for another naked day. At least one more. Remember the timeline: **Clueless** to **I Peed** to **I'm Peeing** to **I have to go pee** .

Still no poop: Okay, so you're on Block Two and you still haven't gotten a poop. Your child may be showing signs of discomfort and/or crankiness. Keep your eyes peeled; you can be sure a poop is coming eventually. **Be watchful when transitioning into pants if you don't have a poop yet.** The illusion of privacy that pants provide is a cue for them to just do it in their pants.

Even on the second day, no poop is very common. It's okay, don't panic. One of the biggest problems with lack of poop is that you, the parent, start to freak out and get anxious. You also start hovering and slip into over-prompting. Head over to the *Poop* chapter for more information.

Full blown tantrums: These are not unheard of in a 2-year-old who is not getting her way. In this particular case, "her way" is a diaper/routine/everything back the way it was. Here's the thing with tantrums: they aren't very satisfying for your child if you aren't tugging at the other end of the proverbial rope. Here's a typical potty training tantrum situation: you prompt her to go pee on the potty. As you are making your way to her, she throws herself down on the floor, immediately becomes either super-rigid or wet spaghetti-ish, starts screaming if you touch her, and... you know the drill. Here's the fix: prompt. As in remind and then walk away. The only reason she's putting on a show is that you are watching, front and center. If you prompt her, leave it at that, and **really** walk away — yes, it sounds risky — you are giving her space and time to make a good decision for herself. If she is busy fighting you, all her energy is being used in fighting you rather than in making a good decision. So, prompt and walk away. Never does a child have a tantrum in an empty room. The nature of the beast is that someone must be watching.

The Bedtime Potty Pit: You know how in the game *Candyland* there are these pits like the Gooey Gum Drop Pit that you can get stuck in? Yeah...in potty training there's a classic one I call the "Bedtime Potty Pit."

It can occur at two possible times: before giving up nighttime diapers, and after giving up nighttime diapers. For brevity, I'll refer to nighttime only, but the same applies for nap time.

It looks something like this: Aaron does great all day long. His mom, Angela, can now trust him to use the potty during the day. He either tells her he has to go or does a really clear pee-pee dance. Daytime is all set. Aaron's bedtime is 7:30. There are the usual three stories and two songs. Dad's in charge of brushing teeth and pjs. Everything looks pretty good, almost out of a *Lifetime* movie. Then Aaron says, "I have to pee." Okay. Pjs off, night diaper off, Aaron sits to pee. Shockingly, there's no pee. Diaper back on. Pjs back on. Tuck Aaron in...almost out of the room. "Pee! I got to pee!" Pjs off. Diaper off. Sit to pee. Hmm. No pee. You can rinse, lather and repeat for...oh...however many times you can imagine. Even better is the poop call, 'cause that just might lead to, let's say, 40 minutes of reading to Aaron on the potty all for a poop.

It's classic. And freaking exhausting. Now, it's 8:30 and well past bedtime, which makes for the most charming behavior. But what do you do? Do you honor the pee and poop call?

I mean, you've done all this hard work, right? What if he means it? But what if he doesn't?

My experience is that the Bedtime Potty Pit (BPP) is a fabulous stall. Aaron has Mom and Dad by the balls, and he knows it. Never in his short life has Aaron had the kind of power he has now. Mom and Dad jump when he says he has to pee. Aaron is not dumb; in fact, he's very smart. He's going to use that power as much as possible, largely for entertainment.

If you're caught in the BPP, give your child three chances (or however many you have predetermined). Let your child know that he has a certain number of chances. You might say something like, "Aaron, this is the last time you will sit to pee. If you don't have to pee, you can hold it until Mommy comes and gets you in the morning." He may or may not pee. You don't want to say, "Last chance or you're stuck doing in it your diapers." At least introduce the notion that he can hold it and that it is up to him. He has a choice: A or B.

The other thing you should do if it looks like your child might use the BPP stall is to start bedtime early enough to factor it in. For Aaron, that might mean starting the whole bedtime routine around 6:45. Remember, this is temporary! You all will find your groove soon enough. If you build in time for the stall, you will be so much less likely to get anxious about it. The stalls are annoying enough on their own, but in addition, we get anxious because bedtime is being put off and we know the kid needs his sleep, or we're stuck with the fallout the next day. So allow yourself plenty of wiggle room.

Don't be afraid of laying down some firm boundaries. Once he has nothing to push against, the game really isn't fun. As always, do this is in a calm, casual manner. Even if he calls out one last time to pee as you're leaving the room, you can say, "Okay, hold it till morning. I love you. Good night." This way, you've acknowledged that you've heard him and that you believe him (even if you don't) but you laid down some boundaries and you're sticking to them. This, my friend, is good parenting.

And you don't have to be concerned if he does pee in his diaper; it's not going to screw with the process. It's a minor behavioral speed bump. Deal with the stall game first, then tackle the nighttime potty training.

Of course, this all gets much trickier without a nighttime diaper, because you have the very real fear that your kid will pee in the bed. You never want to lead with fear! The best thing to do is to leave the potty chair in his room and, after the bedtime routine, say, "Good night. I love you. If you need to pee, your potty is right there." If your child senses you are fearful and unsure, I can guarantee this will become a game for him.

I've found that for the bedtime routine in general, just be sure to leave room for all the antics. Playfully ask her as part of the routine, "Did you have your last glass of water? What shall the last story be? Go for your last pee. Brush your last tooth. Thank you." The one thing that never, ever, ever helps is getting angry or annoyed. This will rile up both you and your child, and you'll accomplish nothing other than to keep the kid awake.

Power struggles: There's another huge issue involved in potty training troubles: the power struggle. Power struggles can make things a little crazy in your house. The average family deals with several power struggles on a daily basis, so potty training power struggles should come as no surprise. Still, it's best to avoid them if possible, which is why it's so important to avoid hovering or over-prompting. Both lead to power struggles.

Should you find yourself facing a power struggle, you need to identify and remove whatever is creating it. This is because — let me be very clear here — you cannot and will not ever win a potty training power struggle with a toddler.

I remember a classic one I had with Pascal. He was about two feet away from me, and I asked him to come over to me in a casual tone. He responded, "No, you come here." I followed with, "No, you come here." We kept going back and forth, and as I started digging in my heels, so did he. Finally, I was able to put on my grown-up brain for a minute and realize we were in fight **about two feet of space**...and I didn't even really need him to come to me! Geez Louise! Come on, Mommy.

Don't even try to tell me that something similar hasn't happened to you. So, as you can imagine, if power struggles can erupt over nothing, think of the power struggle potential of something as big and loaded as potty training! It's a natural hotbed for a struggle.

Also, unlike other potential causes of power struggles, when it comes to potty training, your child truly does hold

THE POWER, in a very literal way. We sometimes feel like our whole world revolves around and is controlled by our kids. The reality, though, is they have no control at all. We tell them where, when, why, and how to do practically everything. This is normal. Their bodily functions, though, are one thing we don't control! They hold the pee (or poop), so they hold the power.

If we look at a power struggle as a tug of war, the absolute best way out of one is to let go of your end of the rope. This does not mean you cave in to what your child wants, it means you let go of your need to control the situation. Most often with toddlers, power struggles arise out of a desire to "do it myself." This is true of potty training as well. Whenever you find yourself engaged in a potty training power struggle, the way you "let go of your end of the rope" is to allow your child to make using the potty his idea. For instance, you could use one of those 'throw away prompts' I have talked about in previous chapters. Prompt and back off. You do not want to hammer home your point or keep repeating the same thing again and again. It won't work and things will escalate.

Too much talking: Yes. Talking to your child is good. And yes, telling your child what you are doing as you are doing it is good. But like all things, talking is good in moderation. There's a current parenting trend that seems to favor a little TOO much talking. Some parents want to explain every little thing, giving a mini-dissertation about everything that happens. Some of this, I think, comes from us trying too hard to teach "actively." Also, some of it — particularly when it comes to potty training — is to mask our own fear.

Here's the thing: as long as you are talking, you are not listening. Also, as long as you are talking, you are not letting your child talk to himself. Self-talk is crucial to language and thought development. Self-talk is what helps your child learn to control his impulses. Self-talk develops with your child and becomes his inner voice. Some experts suggest that children who develop strong self-talk skills make better choices throughout childhood. We may be talking about pee and poop right now but eventually, it's going to be smoking and drugs and sex. With the constant barrage of noise around us in modern society, adding our own voices to the cacophony is not always helpful. When your child talks to himself, he's sorting out all the information he takes in and is making it his own. He's learning to make good decisions FOR HIMSELF. If you are talking, this can't happen.

Furthermore, when you're talking to your child — about potty training or anything else — you're generally also worrying about things along the lines of: "Is he even listening? Or comprehending?" This adds another layer to the talking problem. There's emotion under all that talking. With regard to potty training, that emotion is most likely fear and anxiety (on your part). Children attend to your vibe far above your words.

The bottom line is that most parents talk endlessly to their children about the steps involved in potty training. And most of the time, the kid can recite those steps right back to you. If your child can tell you where the pee and poop go, but he's still peeing on the floor, it's time to stop talking. Instead, use simple directives without a lot of explanation. Then be quiet to give your child room to process the information for himself.

Having trouble with releasing or hating the potty

The Red Solo Cup. Made famous by country music and drinking college students everywhere. It is oh-so-much more than an unbreakable drinking container. It is also a most excellent Insta-Porta-Potty.

Don't laugh, I'm serious.

Now, first off...it doesn't have to be red, nor Solo brand. Any wide mouth, deep container will do. And clearly, this is a better trick for boys...but actually can work surprisingly well for girls, too.

I personally discovered the RSC idea because I have one bathroom. Invariably — and I do mean always — the minute I would sit to pee, my son would announce that he also had to pee. He was well beyond the little potty stage by this time, and I really didn't want to encourage peeing in, say, the tub. So I started keeping a RSC under the sink, tucked away so guests didn't ask questions and no one could mistake it for a drinking vessel.

Here are just a few additional ideas for the Red Solo Cup:

In the early stages of potty training, the cup is great if your child needs some "switching up"; sometimes they start resisting the potty just because they're sick of all the hoopla around it.

The RSC is good if you have a child who's having trouble relaxing and releasing the pee. The cup allows him to focus only on releasing, rather than having to worry about sitting, too.

It is easy to keep a cup in every room, just for emergencies. Remember, at first you only have a few seconds warning to get to the potty.

If your child is resistant to leaving the activity he's immersed in, you can offer the cup as a choice.

If your child is in the tub and announces she has to pee, have the cup handy. Pee is sterile and it's perfectly fine for your child to pee in the tub, but if she is asking, it's best to honor the request and respond. The RSC lets you avoid the whole soaking-wet-transfer to the potty and back to the tub (which usually creates so much commotion that she can't relax and release the pee once she's on the toilet anyway).

The RSC is also handy to keep in the car for a quick pee before arriving to or after leaving from somewhere. (Do yourself a HUGE FAVOR and keep a mason/bell jar with a lid in the car, just in case. At the beach or lake — or in a snowsuit —it's easy to pull out and let your kid do their business with hardly anyone noticing.

Sometimes for kids who are just not loving the potty, the RSC is simply more fun.

As with just about everything I say regarding toddlers, don't overdo it: the RSC is an awesome back-pocket trick, but if you use it too much you could end up with a weird situation on your hands. Because toddlers get weird sometimes (like, always).

Then again, so do country music and drinking college students.

The hover within the prompt: So, you carefully read the two posts in an earlier chapter on prompting and backing off. You feel very confident that you are not over-prompting, but you are still seeing some resistance to your occasional prompts. What's probably happening is that you are hovering after prompting. You may be prompting your child and then standing there, waiting or physically taking him to the potty — depending on his age, you may need to do this, but if he's older than 24 months, you don't — and watching over him to make sure he sits and pees. The trick is to prompt/remind, and then **walk away** (just as you do when you're facing a tantrum). It can feel risky, but you have to leave room for him to make the call. Think of the prompt as a reminder, not as a "make him go" kind of thing. There is nothing for him to resist if you act like you don't care.

As I've stated before, Blocks Two and Three are where it's at. These are the heart of potty training. You should be feeling a sense of progress, even if it's teeny tiny. There may be a day or two during these blocks when it looks like you've stalled out, or even gone a little backwards. That's ok. If you are seeing no progress at all, however, check out the chapters titled *The Reset* and *Behavior vs. Potty Training* before giving up. If your child is under 20 months or over 30 months, be sure to read the chapter relevant to those ages, too.

Chapter 9: Block Four and All the Rest

This chapter is about all the weird little things that can come up late in potty training or after potty training. You never know when some of these might hit, so I'm lumping them all here.

Public restrooms: In one word, gross. I've found a trick that works well for both boys and girls: simply lift the toilet seat and have your child stand on the rim and pee straight down into the toilet. Boys can just pull out their penis, but girls will need to take off panties (when girls are standing with their legs spread to straddle the pot, the pee comes out in a straight shot). This only works for pee, though; there's not much you can do for poops aside from having your child sit. I've tried holding kids behind the knees with their butts sticking out, but this creates too much commotion for most kids. You can also carry mini-packets of sanitizing wipes or travel potty inserts (sold at any major baby store). Also, as I've said, I'm a huge proponent of bringing the potty in the car. Should your child have to go, you're probably not too far from the car. Just remember, whatever you choose to do, that pee is sterile and poop is not.

One additional brilliant tip from a mom: carry Post-Its in your purse. You can use them to cover up the automatic flusher sensor in public restrooms to prevent them from going off while your child is sitting on the potty. Because children are small, it's not uncommon for the flusher to go off mid-poop otherwise. Good luck getting your kid to use the toilet after that.

The bloom is off the rose: This applies if you have a kid who was doing great with the potty and then started having accidents, seemingly out-of-the-blue. The honeymoon is over.

I remember years ago when I quit smoking. The first couple of months were easy. I was so proud and got so much support. If I was bitchy, I could blame it on quitting. Friends checked in daily. But then that tapered off. I had become a non-smoker — a bitchy, fat non-smoker at that — and no one gives you kudos for that. The novelty wore off. The same thing happens with potty training. You think, "He's got this." And he thinks, "I've got this." And as he gets confident, chances are he's just waiting a little too long to get to the potty. Handle it by going back to some watching and prompting.

This is not to say you have to be on your kid like you were in the beginning, but do try to determine what's behind the accidents. A lot of times, kids get very invested in play and forget to go or don't want to miss anything. Sometimes they simply wait too long to go to the potty, and do a little pee-pee in their pants. Or they can't get to a bathroom immediately, and the floodgates open. For ideas how to work around this, see *Random Tips and Questions*.

If your child starts having a lot of accidents out of the blue and there aren't any obvious stressors at home, you might want to look in other places. Is there a new teacher at daycare? Is your child being bullied at daycare? Has his diet changed drastically? Is there something bothering her? Often times, you can just ask your child and she'll tell you.

Gentle questioning and being really aware of all aspects of your child's life will go a long way. Sometimes, something we think is trivial is HUGE in a toddler's life (sometimes???).

I'll use the example of my own son. He was fully trained and then suddenly started having a couple of nighttime accidents a week. At that point, I wasn't even monitoring his fluid intake before bed. He'd wake up to pee if he had to. So this was odd, and I started watching him carefully. I eventually figured out the accidents stemmed from the fact that he had switched daycares. The switch wasn't a big deal to him in and of itself, but the new daycare was more structured than his previous one. The kids only drank fluids at snack/meal time, and even then, only a Dixie cup-full. My son didn't know he could ask for more. Instead, he came home and downed five huge glasses of water. Even potty training all-stars can't handle that kind of fluid intake so late in the day. Once I told him he could ask for water at daycare whenever he was thirsty, he came home and drank a normal amount and the problem was solved. I thought it would be obvious to him to ask for more if he was thirsty, but it wasn't (funny enough, he has no problem demanding more at home).

One final thought on accidents: do not put a diaper back on your child! I cannot state this enough. Once she is potty training, even in the beginning stages, putting a diaper on your child says one thing and one thing only: "I don't trust you. I'm telling you all day that I know you can do it and I have confidence in you. But really, I don't trust you." This is extremely damaging to the whole process. If you don't trust your child, she will never trust herself.

Should your child have an accident, don't punish or berate her. Have her help you clean it up and reassure her that you know she can make it to the potty next time. Of course, this is for the occasional accidents. Severe regressions indicate a big problem that I'll address in *Special Circumstances*.

It's not "okay": This is a sticky point for a lot of parents. You want to make your child feel comforted and accepted, but you must be sure you are letting your child know that it's not okay to pee on the floor. If you are more than a couple of days into potty training and you are still ending up with a lot of pee in places besides the potty, this might be your problem. Many parents don't want to use any negative language or create any negative feelings around about the potty. But the reality is that toddlers only think in black and white; they are incapable of thinking in shades of gray. It's up to you to tell them what is right and wrong. The way you do that with a toddler is through facial expressions, tone and words. At some point in the potty training process, you have to establish that peeing on the floor is bad, and peeing in the potty is good. You must communicate this to your child. How you choose to do it is your parenting call. If you are using the same exact expression, tone and words for pees that do and do not make it into the potty, your child is going to assume that both are acceptable.

Think of it this way: when your child hits another kid, you employ expression, tone, and words to communicate that his action was wrong. You say, "No. We don't hit." You physically intervene and stop the hitting. You most likely will have a frown or a facial expression that communicates displeasure. Same thing with potty training; you don't have to be mean about it, but do be clear. There's a right way and a wrong way. You want to teach your child the right way.

They get it, they lose it, they get it, they lose it: This situation is very similar to the "it's not okay" scenario. Once your child has had a couple of successes in a row, you know he can do it. The learning process is over. Yes, there can still be accidents, but there will generally be some clear reason for them. If there isn't, head over to the *Behavior vs. Potty Training* chapter and give the ideas presented there some thought. Once your child starts to use the potty correctly, you know they CAN. From there, unexplained backsliding is usually a behavioral issue, either the result of resistance or 'laziness.'

Pooping in nap/night diaper: So you're a couple of weeks into potty training and it's coming to your attention that your child is saving his poop for the nap or nighttime diaper. It might appear that she is specifically holding it for her diaper, or it could just look like she has readjusted her timing. Either way, the fix is to ditch the diapers all together. This isn't actually a difficult fix, because most people don't get up in the middle of the night to poop. So you've got nature on your side. Head over to the *Nighttime Training* chapter and start that soon. I highly recommend a couple of nights of bare bummed — not just commando. This is because when your child is sleeping, she needs strong, unconscious reminders to either get up or hold it (in addition to the two wake ups recommended in the chapter). Here's the thing: underpants or commando pj's will help to contain any accident but they can, in fact, actually CAUSE the accident (because fabric on the bum can feel like a diaper and trigger muscle memory). It's a catch-22, and what you decide to do is your call. Regardless, I'd set down some Chux (aka Piddle Pads) or a towel under your child for nighttime. The diaper-pooping issue usually takes one or two nights to straighten out, so it's not like it's going to go on forever once you take the diapers off. Also, giving up diapers all together usually helps clean up any other little potty training issues you may be dealing with.

Revenge pee: Say your child has done something wrong and you've put her in the time-out chair. Once there, she has an accident (but whether it was really an "accident" is unclear). If she's in hysterics, chances are the pee came with the emotion. You might want to attempt to get a pee before the actual time-out (I wish you luck with that). If you get the distinct feeling that the "accident" was more of an "eff you," you can do a couple of things. One, wait until the end of the time-out and then clean it up. I am not a fan of making a child 'sit in it,' and I never recommend it. However, at this age, a time-out shouldn't be more than one or two minutes in any event, so it's not a big deal. You have to have some leverage here; you can't rush to get her out of time-out just because she pees. If you do, you will have accomplished nothing other than to teach her that if she pees herself, she will get out of the discipline. I do advise considering consequences other than time-outs while potty training. To be clear, this is all assuming that the original 'crime' is something like, say, hitting — not potty training-related. If you think you are experiencing bad behavior related to potty training, head over to the *Behavior vs. Potty Training* chapter.

"The inner 'fuck it'": If you have been going at potty training for a few weeks and you are still getting one or more accidents a day on a consistent basis, it's time to go back and do Block One over again. A child having that many accidents doesn't really count as being potty trained. What most likely happened is that something went wrong somewhere along the way, and your child has a gap in his understanding. You don't have to go through the whole process again, but be sure to cover the basics. The problem is this: if a child has a gap in his learning or understanding, he will quickly transition his attitude into what I call "the inner 'fuck it.'" This is the "I don't care" attitude that comes from being stuck and not knowing how to get out of it. Think of the punk in high school who talked back and skipped classes. Nine times out of ten that kid had a learning disorder or other circumstances that interfered with his ability to succeed. The attitude was just a front. The same thing can happen with potty training. We humans like to be good at what we attempt. When we can't do something well, we tend to pretend we don't care about it. Of course, this isn't a logical or conscious thought process, but it's what's going on. Go back and breeze through Blocks One, Two, and Three with your child, and figure out where the gap in learning is (I'm betting it's between being naked and wearing clothes).

So, those are most of the major snafus that can arise in your first month of potty training. There's still a lot more information yet to come in this book, in addition to some really random questions (and their answers) in the chapter cleverly titled *Random Tips and Questions*.

Chapter 10: Poop

Oh Lordy. The big BM. The Grand Dada of Doo Doo. Sometimes it feels like all our effort as parents boils down to getting one freaking poop on the potty. You are not the first, nor will you be the last, parent to be brought to her knees over zee poopage.

So poop makes up an entire chapter of this book, and in it, we're going to delve into a lot of things: society, philosophy, mythology and, yes, actual crap. To make sense of poop, you need to think about your child's perspective and see this through his eyes. There are a few things to keep in mind.

First, all your child has ever known is the feeling of poop right up against his body. Second, as he sees it, no one has ever paid much attention to this very primal, very private function before today. Third, pooping while standing up or squatting is far more natural than pooping while sitting. Fourth, going from pooping in a diaper to pooping in a potty can be freaky as hell. Your patience is required. Your child has no notion yet of the beauty of a clean bum. It's okay; he'll get there.

Think about your poop. You know those gigunda poops? The ones that make you feel like you lost five pounds in one sitting? Personally I love those poops, but imagine how they feel to a small child. Shoot, it must feel like all her insides are falling out. Poops can be scary. To make them a little less so, I encourage parents to let their children empty their own small pot into the big toilet. When you do this, you're going to crack up (or be really grossed out); almost all kids are fascinated by their poop. They will carry that pot to the big toilet staring and smelling and checking out everything about that poop, mostly with a ton of pride: "I did THAT? THAT came outta MY butt? Cooool."

The number one problem with potty training and poop is that kids start holding it in. The other big problem is that they let it out at the wrong time. Unfortunately, the more the child holds it in, the more likely it is to come out at the wrong time. Yeah?

So let's take a minute to dissect the modern poop situation. I'm here to tell you that pooping has gotten more problematic over the past several decades. If your mom wants to tell you about how easy it was for her to get you to poop on the potty, fine. That was then, this is now. We are living in a different world, and we are different parents, yes? I've been potty training kids for at least 14 years. I wrote this book six years ago and started helping massive numbers of people in the last four years. Pooping has become more of a problem lately. I know this.

Also, I'm fascinated with why, in one generation, things have changed so drastically. With why pooping is not only such a big ordeal, but is in fact becoming even more troublesome with each passing year. So I've spent an inordinate amount of time dissecting the poop problem. I will be sharing only the highlights because, seriously...**no one** wants to hear everything I have to say about poops.

Sir Thomas Crapper: This guy is credited with inventing the flushing toilet in the 1800s. Actually, he was a plumber and eventually bought the patent. The real inventor was Sir John Harrington, who invented his first toilet was in 1596. Still, that's pretty useless information, and I'm sticking with Sir Crapper as the dude who invented the potty. It just sounds better. Anyway, the toilet has been around for a pretty long while. Now, I've traveled the globe and have been in countries where squatting and squat toilets are the norm. Let me tell you: squatting is a better way to poop. It turns out there's a reason for this. The anorectal angle (the angle of the tunnel that carries your poop to your anus) gets kinked up upon sitting. When you're squatting or standing, though, there's no kinking. This makes evacuation more than easy; it's almost effortless.

I believe the fact that we (culturally) sit to poop is part of the problem with kids and pooping. We adults have grown very used to it and can deal with it, but for kids, the transition from squatting or standing to poop (which they often do when wearing a diaper) to sitting is highlighted during potty training. By itself, though, this doesn't fully explain the Big Poop Problem. Some kids have no trouble sitting and pooping and, let's face it, the toilet has been around for a long time. If the sitting position were the sole cause of pooping problems, we would've ditched the toilet long before now.

Still, sitting contributes to poop trouble, so until the perfect potty chair is designed — I'm working on it — when your child sits to poop, you can put some books underneath her feet to bring her thighs close to her chest. This helps create proper anorectal alignment, and makes pooping infinitely easier. I personally use a Squatty Potty. You might consider this for yourself and for your child as she gets bigger; my 6-year-old son **loves** it.

In short, the proper poop position is important but it can't be the sole reason for pooping problems.

Pooping is primal: Pooping itself is a very primal function. Our poop is a piece of us - literally - and releasing it requires privacy which, if you think about it, a diaper affords. When a child's bum in covered, it feels concealed and private. It's keeping the bum out in the air, which we do when we potty train, that makes pooping feel public and uncomfortable at first. As adults, we usually go in a small room dedicated to pooping and close the door. We don't take kindly to intruders, either. Our children have those same desires. If your child resists pooping, the very first thing you should offer is privacy. The level of privacy you can give depends on the age of the child. Age also tends to determine how much privacy your child needs. Kids under the age of 24 months generally need less. From 24 months on, each passing month will bring your child more self-awareness. More awareness usually means they need more privacy. Offering your child privacy can be as simple as "forgetting" something in the other room once your child is situated on the potty. Alternately, you can close the bathroom door.

Simply put, too often, especially during potty training, there's a glaring spotlight on a very personal function. But again, that's just one little piece of the pooping puzzle.

Your poop values: What the hell are poop values, right? This is a term I made up to describe your family's view on poop. Do you like poop? Is pooping a joke in your house? (It's better if it is.) When someone goes into the bathroom and leaves a big stink behind, do you talk about the elephant in the room, or do you just not say anything? Are your the sort of family who, when someone farts, everyone pretends it didn't happen? Are you the kind of person who can only poop at home? Simply put, are you embarrassed by poop or is it just one of those things?

In general, we are a culture who disdains poop. Attitudes aside, though, it's a vital bodily function that allows us to eliminate the waste products of our digestion. To quote John Robbins, "You aren't what you eat. You are what you don't shit."

Your poop values are going to be passed on to your child, period. If you don't like poop, your child won't either. If you think it's the most disgusting thing in the world, so will your child. If you can only poop at home, chances are, your kid will be the same way.

None of that is intended as judgment. It's just fact. Some parents are weird about poop, but they expect their child to poop on a potty sitting in the middle of the living room. Yeah. No.

Now, maybe you think you're chill about poop. That's cool. But are you really? A good sign of your true "chillness" is your response to the suggestion that your child be in the bathroom with you while you poop. If you're fine with that (or if that's how it already goes down in your house), great. If you are opposed to the idea, ask yourself why. It's probably a good indication that you're not as chill about poop as you think you are.

I suggest that before beginning potty training, you make it a point to have your child in the bathroom with you while you poop. This is the best way to model the potty behavior you're going to be teaching. Your child can see that pooping might sometimes take several minutes. That people sometimes grunt or make facial expressions. And they see that poop falls out of you, into the toilet, and nobody dies because of it. These are all very valid reasons to have your child see you poop. You don't have to have them with you every time. In fact, it's just as valuable to once in a while announce that you have to go poop and you'd like some privacy. This is a good way to introduce this word and notion.

Diet: Of course, we can't look at pooping problems without talking about diet. Most kids have a pretty clean diet when they're young (generally speaking, I'll say up to about 24 months). Most moms focus on fruits, veggies, and other good stuff. Most moms allow the occasional treat or juice box. After their child turns two, though, I find that most parents start 'caving in' a little more. The number of birthday party invitations increases and, along with them, cake consumption increases. Parents start allowing a little more candy or juice or whatever the case may be. It is, in general, something we all start to relent a little bit more on.

Two years of age is also around the time that toddlers can start to get picky. They start showing food preferences, and it's usually crappy food they prefer. This is the age when the "won't eat anything but macaroni and cheese" phase begins. This is also the age of the on-the-go food. Your child has probably mastered eating without you watching every bite to make sure he doesn't choke, right? So you're more comfortable giving snacks in the car and at the playground. These snacks are generally easy to grab and not horribly messy, like crackers and dry cereal.

Now, I know this isn't a nutrition book, but I'd be remiss if I didn't include a bit about food allergies here in the poop section.

One in 3 of my clients with children with poop problems end up with a food allergy diagnosis. Gluten is the major offender, with dairy being a close second. IF YOUR CHILD IS EITHER OFTEN CONSTIPATED OR HAS LOOSE STOOLS, please, do yourself a huge favor and see an allergist. IF YOUR CHILD IS POOPING LOOSE STOOLS MORE THAN 4x A DAY...something is not right. More importantly, your child is not digesting their food, which can lead to malnutrition.

I know food allergies are a MAJOR pain in the butt. I know this. But I can't tell you the amount of parents who realize a food culprit, fix it and miraculously, their child's poop problem is gone.

And now a few words about fat. The low-fat craze is no good, especially for young children. Be sure your child is getting adequate, healthy fats. Good sources in my opinion are coconut oil, avocado, olive oil, seed and nut butters, high quality butter, and full-fat plain yogurt. Adequate fat will not only help with pooping, but it seems to me that it improves a child's ability to focus and behave.

Personally, I eat according to the Paleo, Primal, or Caveman Diet, and I've never experienced such health as I do now. I don't eat grains and don't feed them to my son. When I switched his way of eating, he became, I swear to God, nearly angelic in behavior. He also is much more focused in school and at home and is not constantly hungry. His bleeding eczema is gone. Again, this isn't a nutrition book, so I'll leave it at that.

If your child is having a hard time with pooping, you may be tempted to up his fiber level. That's fine, but not all dried fruits (a common go-to for increased dietary fiber) are actually high in fiber, and some can have the opposite effect and clog things up (they also stick to tiny molars). Personally, I've found coconut in any form — be it oil, flakes, or milk — to be the **best** for loosening up poops. You can make recipes with coconut, but honestly, just a teaspoon or two of the milk or oil will move things along very nicely. Ground flax seed with coconut milk makes an amazing hot breakfast cereal and really, really helps pooping. Regardless, from my experience, I recommend increasing your child's fat consumption before upping their fiber. Seriously. It makes that big a difference.

All this aside, even diet doesn't completely solve the pooping puzzle. The right diet certainly will help things but it's not the complete answer. After all, it's not like the day you start potty training your child completely changes his eating, right? And still, many parents with a child who pooped three times a day, no problem, with a diaper on see drama start when the diaper comes off. So the trouble's got to be in the potty training.

Here's where things get interesting. I've looked at the poop problem from all angles, trust me. For generations upon generations, pooping has generally not been a problem. Suddenly, the last ten years are bringing about increasing poop problems. Diet is a factor. Squatting versus sitting is a factor. Still, there's one factor we haven't looked at, and in my opinion, it's the big one: the speed at which our world moves. These days, we get information and connect with others so much faster than previous generations ever did. I think the world is moving too damn fast for our kids. I think that as a result, they are anxious, regardless of how we try to individually combat this at home.

If we think of your child as fundamentally anxious, and of the diaper as your child's oldest and dearest security blanket, the poop problem makes sense. In essence, I don't think it's the pooping ITSELF that is the problem. I think our children are clinging to the literal security blanket of something (the diaper) that they've known since birth. Lately, I've seen more and more kids literally asking for a diaper to poop in, as opposed to using the potty. Ten years ago, this was nearly unheard of, and now it's becoming increasingly common

Let's go further and examine the psychology of withholding (not pooping) and its opposite, which is letting go (pooping). As far back as mythology, withholding versus letting go is a very common theme. Even today, that theme drives a lot of movie plots. So if pooping is the Grand PooBah of letting go, why would a child withhold?

I think this is a very interesting question, and worth examining. We, as a society, are on edge. Our politics are damn near a reality show. Our reality shows feed popular culture and promote wildly bad behavior. Facebook has become a very real addiction. Online news, the ability to LIKE and SHARE, blogs...all these things combine to make for a fast-paced world. We as moms, in particular, are subject to an onslaught of not only frightening news (kidnappings, etc) but also parenting media drama, like stupid, jerk *Time Magazine* and the breastfeeding cover. All this media just serves to confuse us and wound our intuition. It also makes us feel anxious, which our children pick up on.

But media isn't the only factor. Children are now a market. That is another big difference I see in comparing a generation ago and now. Birthday parties are big events, and kids get invited to a lot of them. I met a mom who couldn't find a good weekend to start potty training her 2-year-old; six weekends in a row were packed with back-to-back birthday parties. That's too much.

Many, many parents have written me to ask if their child can go to swim class or toddler gym or music class on the second day of potty training. Working potty training into your toddler's schedule is doing things in reverse order. Potty training is a vital life skill; your child needs to learn how to put poop in a potty more than he needs to attend a music class. But that's neither here nor there. The point is, kids these days have busy schedules. We all know that over-scheduling is not good, and we may not think of our toddlers as being truly over-scheduled, but for toddlers, just about anything can count as a big event. I think our children are running on fumes most of the time and have what I call "emotional hangovers."

There's also the fact that parents are highly invested in "making memories." In my opinion, memories get made in the small, lovely moments that take place between you and your child. They don't necessarily require Disneyland or the latest Wiggles concert.

Bottom line, we are moving too fast. We are exposing our children to too much, too soon. It's become part of our society. Case in point, I took my son to the movies to see *Chimpanzee*, a great nature film. He gets to watch TV and go to the movies, but I'm picky about what he watches. The previews at this particular movie nearly gave us both seizures; the speed at which images were thrown at us was assaulting. These days, though, this experience is typical. Everything around us moves at a very rapid pace. We can barely stand boredom; the minute we or our children might be bored, we rush to fill the void.

Now, I live in the real world and I love Facebook and my smart phone, so I'm not suggesting you give up all media, but I am asking you to slow down. Try to combat the overt marketing to our children at home. Take time to revel in their milestones, like potty training, zippering up zippers, tying shoes, and riding bikes. Children love routine. Children need time to discover the world around them. Downtime is not only good, it's essential. Boredom begets creativity; it's good for the soul.

To return to our discussion of poop, I think our fast-paced world is largely responsible for poop problems and why they're so common. I hear from so many moms, "I've been home with my kid for two whole days potty training. I'm going out of my mind." No offense, but spending two days at home shouldn't make you go crazy. Just something to think about.

Be sure you are creating a safe haven for your child, so she has room to slow down and explore at her own pace. We have it all backwards today. We are overstimulating and over-scheduling, and despite this, we are delaying life skill milestones.

My son's preschool was fantastic. They were very Montessori/Waldorf-y but had no official affiliation with either. They baked their own snacks every day and sat family-style. They poured their own water and measured stuff. No characters were allowed, to discourage marketing to children, no sugar was allowed in their lunch boxes — that kind of school. One of the reasons I choose this school was because there was no play yard. The school was located downtown, and the kids utilized the entire city around them. They went out every single day of the year — except for one very blizzard-y day — cold, rain, shine, or snow. I highly valued that.

They also taught the kids how to completely dress themselves for the weather. How to get on snow pants and mittens and boots. How to zipper and button and tie. It was fantastic!! This teaching of life skills was so much more valuable than any other sort of "teaching" they could have done. Let me tell you: we live in New England, and having a 3-year-old who can get his own winter clothes on is truly an amazing thing. I bring this up because to me, that's the right order of things. My child's brain didn't need specific stimulating for math or reading or music. My child needed to be in control of his own person. Learning life skills like how to use the potty lets that happen. It builds inherent self-pride in mastery. That's where self-esteem grows.

What do to about the pooping: All this chatter about why pooping has gotten harder is all well and good, but you're here because you want to know what to do about it, so let's look at the most common scenarios and some super-special ones too.

As we do so, something to keep in mind above all else: this is **all new**. The feeling of warm, squishy poop next to your child's bum is the norm. A free-falling poop into "a pit" of sorts can be scary. It's our social norm to put our poop in a container but remember, for the better part of two years, your CHILD'S norm has been the diaper.

Here are two blog posts I wrote about poop drama:

—————————————— *From the Blog* ——————————————

Poop.

Poop. Poop. And more poop.

*All we have done as mothers and humans —
graduate school, careers, global travel, making art,
making life — all to culminate in us being brought
to our knees because our child did or did not poop in
the potty. Had someone told you five years ago that
you'd be here now, you'd probably have laughed out
loud. But here it is. Poop. The begging. The cajoling.
The eagle-eye for signals. If you have cried over
poop, this post is for you.*

*You are not the first, nor will you be the last, to have
poop on the brain. Poop is an endless topic in potty
training — everything from slight, unconscious
withholding, to willful pooping on the floor, to
massive power struggles over requesting a diaper in
which to poop. If you are registered on our forum,
you know the topic list reads: Poop. Poop. Poop.
Poop. Poop.*

*There are so many facets to why pooping is so
dramatic that I've broken the topic down into
digestible parts. Let's take a few minutes and talk
about the many things that are going on during
your basic poop in the potty. Part One of this Poop
Series — really, did you ever, in your life, think you'd
be reading a Poop Series on a blog? — is the slight,
unconscious withholding. This is a huge concern for
a lot of parents. It might look like this: your child
used to poop two or three times a day in a diaper.
Now you officially start potty training and...no poop.
There may be resistance to actually sitting on the
potty. Some children will say a variation of, "my bum*

hurts." Or she may say nothing, and there's just no poop.

The number one thing you need to remember, right from the get go, is that poop is personal, in a very primal way. I think we as adults understand that when it comes to ourselves, but somehow we forget it when it comes to kids. Poop is one of the few things we can truly call our own. Here's another way to look at it: it's said that the mouth and teeth are highly emotional, which is why so many people panic at a trip to the dentist. It's an orifice. It's mine. Don't go in there. Right? Well that's an orifice everyone can see, for gawd's sake! The butt hole was not meant for scrutiny. And yet, here we are all up in our kids' business and what they keep up there. This whole process was kept tucked away in a diaper — of course, you did change the diaper, but you had no part in how the poop came out, right? You had no idea how the process worked for your kid. You probably saw a 'poop face,' but that's just when it got pushed out. We have no idea how long it took to "park itself on the off ramp." So now you start potty training and it's like this glaring spotlight has now been put on your kid's butt and what it produces.

Let's take another minute to talk about that glaring spotlight on an otherwise, private function. The anus is a sphincter muscle. It opens and closes with emotion. [This is one of my favorite lines from my book — I'm even thinking of getting t-shirts made. Because I am not well.]

I'll give you an example by way of another big sphincter muscle: the cervix. The cervix is one of the major muscles responsible for a baby's journey out into the world. Ina May Gaskin, a world-renowned midwife, explains how the cervix needs to be open to effectively give birth. She also notes that it can slam shut:

"Even when the voluntary muscles get tired, the sphincters don't get tired. Those are connected to the organs that fill up with something; the bladder, uterus, intestines. They expand and contract, and when they yawn open, whatever is inside comes out, and then they close again. But, they work better in privacy; they're shy, and this is true of humans and most animals. We seek privacy to allow our sphincters to do their jobs, jobs that at the most basic level, have to do with hormone levels in the body. For example, oxytocin levels in blood rise when something big comes out (whether it's a baby or a bowel movement). Laughter is one thing that can help open the sphincters. I ask women to laugh when they're having a baby because it helps the process along; it also adds to oxytocin and endorphin levels. But on the converse, if someone is afraid or feels violated, for example, the sphincter can slam shut."

Now, she has been known to illustrate this point in her birth classes. She puts a big silver bowl in the middle of the room, with a hundred dollar bill in it. Anyone who can poop in the big silver bowl can have the $100. So far, no one's been able to.

So, here we are potty training and the potty chair is pretty much in the middle of the room — even if only metaphorically speaking — right? The spotlight is on the potty chair. The spotlight is on the child and the poop. We're expecting the child to poop in the silver bowl...and it doesn't always work that way. The tricky part is that you can't give your child complete privacy when they are learning something. They can't be left alone because they most likely need your help in recognizing the feeling of needing to poop and manipulating the actual getting to and on the potty chair.

I generally find parents are not tolerant of any stalling on the child's part, when it comes to poop. The parents have decided to potty train, and expect everything to just flow the way it did in the relative privacy of the diaper. When things don't flow that smoothly, the parents confuse the delay with the child 'not being ready.' In fact, the complete opposite is true: the earlier you potty train, the less your child is aware of the general need for privacy during this bodily function. The older child will be very aware, and will thus show increased resistance.

As the cervix does, the anus relaxes in an environment that is gentle. An environment without a lot of fanfare and words. An environment that is relaxes, semi-private, and perhaps filled with laughter. The more normal and routine you can make pooping for your child, the more relaxed the anus is going to be. The glaring spotlight of this whole process can back some kids up (not to the point of true constipation, but to where they're not pooping the normal once or twice a day). That's totally normal. The analogy to labor carries through: when you are in labor you want someone sure and steady by your side. You don't want someone over-talking logic and reason. You don't want someone high-strung. And you certainly don't want anyone breathing down your neck to get it done.

Patience, consistency and understanding are what will make this normal for your child. I realize providing privacy is hard with a small child who is just learning a new skill, but there are some ways you can help. In the very beginning stages of potty training, I suggest you keep the potty chair wherever your child spends the most time, but that doesn't mean it has to be in the middle of the room. The pooping process can be discreet without being behind closed doors. You can be by your child's side but not all up in his business (Seriously. Do not spread your kid's butt cheeks to check if the poop is coming. A hard urge to resist, but resist you must.) A really great trick is to get your child sitting for a poop and all of sudden think of something you need to do in the other room. Tell him to sit tight, you'll be right back. Nine times out of ten, the child will poop when you are gone for a minute. In fact, a huge telltale sign that it's time to potty train right now is when your child goes somewhere specifically to poop. Don't miss that window of opportunity!

The goal is to take that glaring spotlight off your kid and off this process. No one wants to poop with all eyes on them. Of course, a nice poopy dance once the deed is done is perfectly fine!

If your child isn't pooping in those first few days, relax. This isn't willful and it's not manipulation: it's a normal process of wanting to keep what's theirs, theirs. Of course, this is just one minor component to the Drama of the Poop. I'm sure you'll be waiting for Part Two with bated breath. Scintillating stuff, poop.

Part Two:

So in Part One, I quoted Ina May Gaskin. Towards the end of her discussion of sphincter muscles she says, "...if someone is afraid or feels violated, the sphincter will slam shut." Of course, she's referring to the cervix and birth and I'm referring to the anus and poop. Same diff. A sphincter by any other name is still a sphincter.

Now, that brings us to the next logical point. Why on Earth would a child feel afraid or violated during potty training? Well, for a lot of reasons, actually, none of which have to do with 'readiness.' I already mentioned the privacy issue: putting a glaring spotlight on a private function can feel violating. Of course, I'm not talking about the kinds of horrible violation that you sometimes see on the news — I'm

talking more the embarrassing kind of violation
— but nonetheless, on a primal level, it can feel
violating. The same kind of embarrassing feeling of
violation that makes us not want to blow a bunch of
farts when we're in a public restroom and someone's
in the next stall. I know you know what I'm talking
about.

So, let's look at why a child might be afraid of
pooping on the potty. For starters, it's new. Toddlers
are known routine-lovers. Diapers have been their
routine since...hmmm...about two hours after birth.
Think about that. Your child may well have been in
a diaper before he even fed for the first time! Wow.
It's pretty crazy when you look at it, huh? So yeah,
something this big and new is going to throw him.
You know how most kids go through a period of
separation anxiety when they're apart from you?
Well, they've known and loved a diaper about as long
as they've known and loved you. So it's fair to say the
fear can be equated with a sort of separation anxiety.

I use many phrases to describe what a diaper might
mean to a kid: a habit, a routine, an addiction,
a security blanket. Behind the words is the same
notion: pooping in a diaper is all your child has
known. Now, you and I logically know about waste
management, the toxicity of fecal matter and the
wonders of the sewer system, but once again, let's
look at this through toddler eyes: since the dawn of
your kid's time, he has pooped in a diaper. Maybe he
knows you go elsewhere to do your business, maybe

he knows you don't wear a diaper, maybe he knows other grownups go elsewhere to do their business. But probably not. Because toddlers don't really give a crap about anyone but themselves, as witnessed by the never ending required messaging, "Please share." This is all totally normal and, I think, kind of cool. Anyway, all this is by way of saying: don't expect your toddler to come to the logical conclusion that one day, he too will be pooping in that same designated place. In fact, expecting anything logical at all from your toddler would be your first mistake.

So your kid, for probably around two years, has been pooping the only way he knows how, and then one day, you ask him to poop elsewhere. Do you see how this could be met with resistance? Imagine if you came to visit me at my house and I told you that we only poop in the corner of my living room. I tell you up, down and sideways that it's okay. We all do it. Really. I'll give you privacy. Please, please, poop in the corner of my living room. Don't worry! I'll clean it up! No matter what, it would still feel wrong. Am I right or am I right? Because you know logically that it's unsanitary, and you have long been conditioned to poop in the proper place.

Ahhh...conditioned to poop in the proper place. How do you condition a small human, whose logical reasoning is not developed? Funny you should ask. I'll take consistency and repetition for $1000. That is the name of the pooping game, guys, consistency and repetition.

Why else might your child be afraid of pooping in the potty? If you are eating while reading this, you might want to stop for a bit.

Look, all your child has known — in addition to a diaper — is the warm, cozy feeling of her poop against her butt. That feeling is her normal. It's her safe, her routine. It seems pretty gross to us as grown ups, but it feels really good to kids. Mostly, because it's all they know. I've actually worked with kids who can say outright, "I like the warm feeling of my pee and poop in my diaper." Good thing they're cute, huh?

And of course, let's not forget the fear of the toilet itself. Over the years, I've heard of every manner of monsters that live in the toilet. It's all fun and games to flush until it's time to actually put their own tushies there. Again, looking through the kids eyes: they don't understand where the toilet flushes to (dang logic). And then we ask them to expose a very personal, vulnerable part of their anatomy this gaping chasm of God-knows-what. So yeah, it can be scary. Some children will parlay that fear right over to the little potty, but most kids get a real kick out of seeing just what and how much they produced (which can be freakishly large) and dumping it in the toilet. This is why I always recommend a little potty chair; I think they are brilliant. The little pot keeps the poop at least semi-close. It's a literal way for them to see what came out of them. It can be scary to give up what feels like a big of yourself and not have it close by, at least for a while.

I also think the little potty chair is tremendously useful in getting the right amount of squat to properly evacuate. If your child is having trouble pooping on the big toilet insert, you should try the little potty chair with books under his feet.

So all in all, when you are potty training, you're redirecting a life-long habit. It may be a short life thus far, but still, a life-long habit. As with so many habits that are instilled for any length of time, it's best to stop the habit cold turkey. Have you tried to get a kid to stop sucking on a binky? What works is throwing the binky out and dealing with the fallout, if there is one. Do you think it would effective to let the child have the binky for an hour in the morning but no other time? Probably not. Toddlers don't think logically. They don't know time. Same thing with diapers. Many parents take the fear or resistance as a sign that the child is not ready; this is not true. In fact, the longer you keep your child in diapers, the longer this habit gets entrenched, the more attached the child is to the habit, the more normal the warm feeling of pee and poop against his skin becomes. It becomes harder and harder with passing time to get the kid to give this up. The resistance and fear actually increase, which is what leads to epic power struggles.

*The whole point of this Poop Series is to try to get you
to understand and thereby have some patience with
the drama around pooping. It's not meant to cause
you to over-think and over-analyze potty training
(let me do that for you). It's not meant to make you
tiptoe around your child or the process. The best way
to potty train is in one fell swoop: do it, done. I'm
writing all of this because we're grown ups and we
forget. I encounter a large number of people who are
very concerned that they not start potty training too
early and yet, once they begin, they want it done in
140 characters or less. Start it at the right time and
chances are you won't have to deal with any of this in
the first place. Seriously.*

Not getting any poop at all: This problem has many
different forms. The first couple of days, we can't really make
a call. As I've stated many other places in this book, the first
few days are learning. We can't say for certain what's going
on until we see a pattern emerge. IT'S VERY COMMON for
your child not to poop on the first or second day of potty
training. There's a lot of pressure, even from the most chill
parents, and there's some performance anxiety. This natural
pressure is why we want to keep everything low-key and
relaxed. Within this broad category of "no poops" there are a
few variations.

If your child seems be doing fine with peeing and attempting
to sit to try to poop, don't worry at all about the poop. It will
come.

If your child is clearly doing a poop dance — you know they have to go, they know they have to go and they sit, pop up, sit pop up, walk on tiptoes and the like — it's okay. Don't try to rush them. I've seen this dance go on for up to 10 hours. Reassure them that poop goes in the potty. Always use words like "let go," "slide," "let it out," "drop" – think *passive* words. For kids, poop usually does tend to slide out and, in fact, they are doing much more work by holding it. Remind them that they can use either the little pot or the toilet insert. Some kids have a clear preference. Offer to read to them or just sit with them. Remember this is a new sensation. It can be freaky because it's **new**. This dance and poop troubles never have anything to do with 'readiness'. Most often, the poop will come in due time and it will land in the potty or toilet.

What if the poop dance has gone on and on and on and of course, the minute you aren't watching, it lands on the floor? This is okay for the first one or two poops. Well, it's not okay actually, but it's not going to derail the process. Just remind your child that it's not okay to poop on the floor and that poop goes in the potty. Validate the feelings. "I know it feels very strange and you must put your poop in the potty." If your child seems weirded out by the poop, you always want to validate that feeling. You are never, ever going to convince her that it doesn't feel strange or at the very least, new.

If the poop comes the minute you turn your back — usually this poop is also done in the corner — this is great news. This child simply needs more privacy. As I mentioned in the blog posts above, you can get him situated on the potty and the "forget" something in the other room. Nine times out of ten the poop will come when you are out of the room.

I'll mention this again later on, but often times when a kid is doing an elaborate poop dance (walking around holding her butt, usually on tippy toes, and it's very clear they have to go) the best approach is actually one of backing off. You can just throw out there, "I can tell you have to poop. There's your potty, or you can use the big toilet." This is a perfect time to be sure you are not over-talking. You need to give her some room to make a good decision.

If you have done all of this and you are consistently getting poops in the pants or the floor, it's time to amp things up a bit. One thing that can really help is actually having your child help you clean up. Obviously, don't let your child handle the actual poop. But have him go get clean clothes and change himself. Take your time about it. The idea is that it should start to register that it takes a lot more time out of play to clean up than to just sit and do it on the potty. You don't want to let your child dump the poop and flush it down. That's the part of the process that is usually fun and he doesn't get to do that unless he sat for the whole deal.

The next thing you might need to do is provide a small, immediate consequence. Some parents balk at this. You do not want to give consequences in the first couple of days, when your child is still learning but after you are pretty certain she knows the ropes, at least in theory, it's okay to give a small consequence. As I said, it should be small and immediate. Usually taking away whatever she is playing with at the time, or taking her out of that activity, does the

uts are usually ineffective, as are longer term
ces, like taking away dessert after dinner. Little
i have the thought process to connect such separate

The reason you want to give a consequence is that, once he knows the drill and is still pooping in his pants or on the floor, you're dealing with a behavior issue. Whether it's intentional rebelliousness or just being 'lazy,' it's still behavior. The consequence shouldn't be mean or draconian, but should simply reinforce cause-and-effect in a way that actually affects him. When pooping in his pants isn't enough of an effect (and for some children, it isn't) we need to add another component. You can also refer to the *Behavior vs. Potty Training* chapter for more on this.

When I met former client Rachel, her son was pretty well potty trained. He would pee on his own, but pooping in his pants was a recurring issue. Rachel really balked at giving a consequence. To her, it felt wrong to "punish" her son, Sean. Upon further discussion with her, it became clear that Sean fell into the 'lazy' category. He just didn't want to leave his activity. She tried pausing the activity to encourage him to use the potty — no dice. She tried bringing a toy to the potty — no dice. She even tried having him help clean up, but since he couldn't really touch the poop, it didn't seem to faze him. When I suggested a consequence, she fought me tooth-and-nail. She didn't see the difference between a consequence and a reward, and she preferred to reward rather than punish.

I'll tell you what I told Rachel, and what I'll say in the book many times: I don't believe in rewards for expected behavior. If you want to give it a go, that's fine. I've personally seen it create much more trouble than good. I don't think a sticker or a little candy is enough to change a behavior. I also don't think sticker charts work. I don't think a child has the thought process to say, "Oh, I have four stickers this week; three more and I get a prize." I've seen kids learn to meter out pee and poop to get more rewards and I've seen candy create bigger power struggles during potty training. It's not worth it. Occasionally, I will see a kid who I can't quite figure out — has he actually learned it or not? — and even in that case, a small consequence can help. Again, this doesn't require being mean. It's just a way of bumping up the child's level of caring about learning the new skill.

Rachel ended up taking away a small toy every time Sean pooped in an inappropriate place. It wasn't drama filled or anything; just a "you do this and I do that" bumping-up of consequences. Within two days, Sean was pooping on the potty just fine. For whatever reason, he just needed that extra external motivation. I'll say more about this in the *Behavior vs. Potty Training* chapter.

If several days have gone by and you are not getting any poop at all, it's very important to clean your child out. I highly suggest a small dose of some mild stool softener. Pedialax, Metamucil, Miralax, milk of magnesia...anything along those lines. I suggest starting with a half of the recommended dose at first. We just want to soften things up, not create a mess. "Poop foods"(high fiber-ish) are fine as well, but often don't have quite the same effect as a stool softener, and if you over-do them, some can be constipating.

I know many moms have successfully used suppositories. I used to think suppositories were an "end-of-the-line" extreme measure. Slowly, more and more moms were reporting back to me that they used suppositories to GREAT effect. It's something to consider if you are having trouble with a child holding. Two things I think are great is that 1. suppositories have no side effects and 2. the poop comes within 15-30 minutes. Often a stool softener can take up to a day to work it's magic and still more often, can create a poopy mess.

The big problems with backed-up poop are that: a) it will get hard and create some pain when it finally does come, and; b) it can really press up against the bladder, causing many more pee accidents.

Past rectal pain or any butt trauma: Consider whether your child has had any sort of rectal pain before. I've worked with all kinds of kids who've had all kinds of butt trauma. Some kids have constipation from an early age. Some kids have needed surgery on their genitals or anus. Some kids have had blood in their stools. If your child has had any kind of rectal pain or butt trauma, naturally we want to take potty training slow and easy. Always start potty training with some sort of stool softener. You absolutely want the first potty training poops to be easy ones. Always validate to your child that you know he has had a hard time in the past. Try not to ever use the word "hurt". Once a child associates that word with the potty and starts using it, it's very hard to ascertain if he is truly in pain or just don't want to go. The word "hurt" is the quickest way to get straight to your heart. Instead, I use phrases like, "had a hard time," "it's been uncomfortable," etc. We don't want to add any emotional charge to this process.

For kids with trauma, you can't convince them that it's going to be easy. They know it has hurt in the past and that's all they know. This is when a little Mommy Magic can go a long way. Much as the placebo effect of your kiss heals most wounds, we can use your Mommy Magic here for poop. You can give the stool softener in juice (this works well with prune juice) and call it Magic Poop Juice. You can cast a "magic spell" around the potty chair or with a wand on your child's head. "My poop slides out, I flush it down. I'm the smartest girl in town." or something similar. If your child will let you, you can put some Vaseline or coconut or olive oil around her anus. Call it Magic Poop Lotion. Any other "magic" you think will resonate with your child is worth a try to smooth this process.

These suggestions may sound utterly ridiculous to you, but I assure you, they work wonders. I've had lots of kids drink the Magic Poop Juice down and declare within minutes that they have to poop. What's important to remember is that they're dealing with a made-up fear turned into a real one, so any way you can dispel the fear is good.

Your child is really trying to make it to the potty but is one second and a half a loaf too late: This kid is awesome and we have to give him props for trying. He just needs to recognize the feeling a little sooner. You can help him by showing him — drum roll, please — The Really Gross and Really Effective Playdough Poop Trick:

I swear to God...

One of the biggest problems with kids and those first few poops on the potty is they can't see what's going on. The feeling hits and a chasm is opening and it freaks them the hell out.

So, here's a little trick that I find helps kids visually connect the feeling with what's happening. When they have this visual it clicks: "Ooooh...so when this happens, I need to get to the potty." This is great for kids who seem to be doing their best to get to the potty, but are not quite making it. You can also use it for the kid who dances around for 10 hours, hops on and off the potty, and still seems weirded out by pooping.

Get yourself some playdough. Bonus points if you use brown. Make a fist. The spot where your thumb curls around your index finger is a reasonable facsimile of the anus. Tada! Now your visual is ready. Put the brown playdough in your fist and squeeze some out. Yep. Totally gross. Kids love it. Explain to them, "When your poop is here (tucked inside your fist) but wants to come out, you tell me. When your poop is here (squeezing out of the fist), it's already out and it's too late." If you feel really brave you can explain what all happens with the anus opening.

This is usually very fun and informative for the child. For most kids, a total light bulb goes off for them. And for you, it's yet another parenting moment of thinking, "Never in my life would I have seen myself doing this."

Your child is doing great with pee but seems afraid of pooping: This child is doing mostly great but the poops keep landing in her pants or on the floor. I just want to be very clear, because the distinction is important: this child is not afraid of *pooping*. This child is afraid of *pooping on the potty*.

The number one thing to remember in the case of this child is that the fear is real for him. As with any other fear — the monster under the bed, water, or whatever — no amount of convincing on your part is going to change his mind. So stop trying.

If you're dealing with this child, you have a parenting call to make, and I do not feel comfortable advising exactly what to do because it will depend upon your child, and you know your child best. What I can do is to give you some ideas. Most often, I tell parents to do what they would do with any other toddler fear. If your toddler fears a monster under the bed, you don't keep her up all night, right? You probably combine some sternness with some magical thinking (like using a stuffed animal sentry or a "No More Monsters" spray). Same idea applies to potty training. Having your child's stuffed animal use the potty first seems to work miracles. Also, having your child on the potty in the bathroom while you are going works well, too.

Phew. That's a lot of pooping information. Come back to this chapter later if you need to. Don't try to digest this all info if it's your first time through the book. The biggest deal with poop is that you have to be calm, regardless of what your child is doing. Remember: the opposite of 'holding it' is letting go. Make it safe for your child to let go. That means you stay calm and steady.

Chapter 11: Prior Attempts At Potty Training

Over the years I've been called upon more and more to fix potty training attempts gone awry. Most people run into trouble because they've waited too long or have been too casual about it.

This chapter is for you if you've made any attempt at all to potty train, and it hasn't gone well. I want to be clear: I'm not saying this is your fault. Still, you've probably made some classic mistakes if your potty training hasn't been successful.

Often with my clients, I'm not called in until the entire process has disintegrated into a huge disaster. Parents' nerves are frayed, if not completely shot. Kids are ridiculously resistant: pooping on floors, running and screaming from the potty chair, disrespecting and ignoring parents (who, to be fair, are pretty hysterical). I've seen it all and I am not exaggerating. I know this is shocking, but potty training elicits all kinds of emotions from both your child and you. Still, sometimes what looks like chaos — once pulled apart — is a relatively easy fix.

While every child and every situation is slightly different, I have divided troublesome trainings into four main categories, which I'll label only to give you a clearer idea of what you are working with:

1. Kind of potty trained
2. Mostly potty trained
3. Clueless
4. The "child from hell"

So let's go through each category and figure out what went wrong and how to fix it.

The kind of potty trained child: This most often results from a "let's just put out the pot" or a "we're just being really casual about this" attitude. Translation: you haven't really committed. Once you commit to potty training, your child's abilities will follow in short order.

Where to go from here? Just pick a day and begin. Follow all the instructions in Chapter 5. This child is just waiting for you to show up with consistency. It doesn't much matter what the specifics are.

Maybe you haven't committed because he hasn't really shown much interest. To this, I say, he may **never** show that much interest. My son didn't show any interest in learning to tie his shoes. In fact, he said he didn't want to. I bought only tie shoes and he learned. **It came down to the fact that I knew he was capable**. Don't make the mistake of waiting for your child. There's a great quote I keep hearing from parents again and again: "Wow. It's like he was just waiting for me to take off the diapers." Yes. Your child expects you to take the lead in life. It's good.

The "kind of potty trained" child is an easy fix. With consistency and repetition, this child should be done in a short amount of time, as long as you just pick a day and start in with Block One.

The mostly potty trained child: This kid is a little harder. The biggest problem here is that no one knows exactly what's going on in this kid's mind. She knows what to do and when to do it and mostly does it just fine. However, she can hold pee and/or poop until she has a diaper on (naps and bedtime). She may even request a diaper to poop in.

As best I can tell, this scenario is the result of waiting too long, though you most likely are not doing anything wrong right now. It's possible that you may have a power struggle on your hands in this case, but not usually. No, this one we can generally chalk up to toddler weirdness. After about 2-and-a-half years, toddlers come up with any number of bizarre fears. The beloved vacuum becomes a source of terror. The bed becomes a home for monsters. The dark all of sudden becomes scary. And, not surprisingly, the toilets holds all kinds of dark secrets that toddlers want no part of. Sometimes, peeing and pooping — for some unknown toddler reason — becomes something "not to do."

For this child, it's absolutely best to just give up ALL diapers. You can go back and breeze through the blocks of learning. It might be helpful to see if she is successful with the potty while naked, and the trouble comes when you try to put clothes on her. I would definitely review the *Poop* chapter. Still, you really have no other option but to ditch the diapers. There will most likely be some fighting and some dancing around, but in the end, it's worth the struggle.

A lot of parents feel like they are traumatizing the child by taking the diapers away — they're not. I've mentioned before that I've had clients whose kids were kicked out of kindergarten for not being properly trained. They had to poop while at school and could only poop in a diaper they requested. They were asked to leave. That, to me, is truly traumatizing. Avoiding that trauma is worth a weekend of struggle.

Most often, poop is the problem for this child, not pee. A good approach is to give a mild stool softener and say, "We are not using **any** diapers anymore. You should poop during the day on the potty, like Mommy and Daddy do."

This child is almost always older and quite articulate. No matter what, you should ask your child what she thinks the problem is. I've heard kids say wild things: "There's a shark transformer in the toilet bowl and if I poop he's gonna come eat my butt" is just one example. It's good to find out what your child is thinking. Even if it seems absurd to you, it is totally valid to your child. You may simply have to reassure your child that nothing bad is going to happen if they poop or pee in the toilet.

Make sure you're not pressuring your child. This problem will not be solved by any amount of begging, bargaining, asking or logic. You also want to check in with your poop values. Remember those? Your "poop values" are how you feel about pooping. If you're sending the message that pooping is the most disgusting thing on the planet, your child probably will have an issue with poop.

Bottom line, make the "new way" (no diapers) an absolute, regardless of the emotional fallout. I often take this out of the potty training context to explain it better. Say you have to suddenly move. You don't want to move, nor does your child, but you have to move next week. **You can't change that**. You can only move forward and do your best with the resulting behavior. With this child and potty training, you want to take that same approach. You have to KNOW that continuing diapers could potentially lead to even more trouble down the road. This is the new way. Period.

The clueless child: This child shows no indication of knowing what the hell you are talking about when you say "potty." Assuming there are no emotional or developmental delays, the truly clueless child is probably too young (which isn't to say it can't be done, just that it will just take longer). Remember, the truly clueless will pee as she is walking, slip on the pee, and still not know what the hell just happened. The flip side of the "clueless and too young" child is the "clueless and too old" child. If your child is over three years of age and appears to be clueless, she is pretending. She is under the impression that if she ignores potty training, it will go away.

If your child is under 22 months and shows **absolutely** no indication that she knows what's happening, you might want to try again in a month or two. Be careful though. Make sure this isn't just an excuse on your part. Make sure there's really **no** indication; she's truly clueless. Go back to Chapter 2 and review the "markers" that I discussed. If your child shows even the slightest indication that she knows what's happening, you should move forward with potty training. You may have to work a little harder or be a little more vigilant but you shouldn't give up.

A very different species is the "clueless" older child. This child will appear deaf to prompting, may completely ignore you, and pretty much act like he's never heard the word "potty" before in his life. In this case, you should refer to the *Younger than 20 months, older than 3 Years* chapter.

I've seen this scenario fixed in half a day and I've seen it take two days, so be prepared. Don't be afraid to enlist someone's help. Sometimes, you (the parent) are too enmeshed emotionally. Have a friend, babysitter, or grandma help out. Results are usually quicker with someone else, just because our kids like to drive us crazy.

Whatever you do, when you decide it's time for potty training to happen, **you can not go back to diapers**! And be very, very careful not to threaten that you will go back to diapers. This child can be working your very last nerve. Be sure you are giving good attention and love elsewhere. I've seen parents get very resentful and be sort of bitchy all the time with this type of kid. All the more reason to clean it up once and for all.

The child from hell. This child is the best of the worst. He is similar to the "clueless" older child except he's waaaay more vocal about wanting potty training to disappear. This child is almost always older than 3, and he means business. He WILL NOT potty train.

Something happened along the way during potty training, the result of which is that he has decided not to play along with you. It could have been anything, big or small. I wouldn't waste too much time going over what you may or may not have done. The most important thing to remember is that kids age 3 and up are **fully capable of understanding all aspects of potty training**. He isn't saying no because of mixed messages or confusion. He is saying no to piss you off and/or assert his will. This situation requires immediate action, because this child is cutting off his nose to spite his face — just to prove he can.

With the "child from hell", you have a true power struggle. He knows where pee and poop go. He is aware of the feeling of having to go. He is aware of the frustration and drama he is creating. Consequently, it's time for you to be a little hardcore. This child needs no coddling, praise or other accolades around potty training. Basically, he's saying, "Fuck you."

It's wise to keep in mind that this situation (or, the resultant power struggle) is rarely about potty training. This is about who is running your house. And I bet if you've gotten to this point, it's not you who's running the show. I'm not saying that to cast blame or judgement. Our kids are constantly walking this line, and we can lose control without even realizing it.

If this sounds like your situation; first, take a deep breath and be kind to yourself. This happens sometimes, and the idea is to fix it, not ruminate on how it got that way. On the other hand, I'm going to be hardcore with you. Things have to change now, for reasons of dignity. Your child is too smart and too old to be using a diaper, period. And if your child is using this as a method of being disrespectful to you in any way, you want to change that now!

Logistically speaking, you'll be hard pressed to find a preschool or kindergarten that will accept an untrained child.

Also, it almost goes without saying, but do you want your child to learn to use the potty through shaming by his peers? Four- and 5-year-olds are already starting to tease, taunt and call names. What do you think is going to happen to your child who's still not trained? It won't be pretty.

This child requires the big guns; a combination of all our tools. When it does become time to train, he's probably too big for the little potty chair, so go right for the toilet. I would give this child the benefit of the doubt that there could be a gap in learning, so go ahead and proceed through the blocks as described earlier in the book, but do so at a fast pace. Because in reality, this is probably just a behavior issue. Still...it's good to be sure.

You definitely want to ditch all the diapers at once. There just can be **no other option**. You also want to utilize silence. Your child has you wound tight right now. I'm sure you have tried everything. So now, try nothing. Stop the dance around him. You may need to stay home and keep your child home for a few days. There will most likely be a full day of accidents but again, there's only so far a kid will go when there's no show around it. What's the point of consistently peeing yourself when Mom doesn't react?

If your child is pooping on the floor, I want to emphasize that this isn't about potty training — it's simply total disrespect. If this is happening, as I discuss further in Chapter 15, you probably need more specific help than I can offer via this book. I would honestly and gently say you may need a family therapist. You have a bigger issue than just poop.

Assuming no greater looming psychological issues, though, if you can manage to stay absolutely neutral for a day or two, your child should get on board. I cannot stress this enough: it's your reaction that is fuelling your child (who, to be fair, is being a pain in the ass, so cut yourself some slack).

The "child from hell" is an expert at appearing to not care about anything. Rewards, punishments...nothing seems to affect him — which is absolutely infuriating. A good way to deal with this situation is to think, "What is she getting from this?" There's always a pay-off when a child acting out of control, be it physical or emotional. Think of what your child's pay-off is, and remove it.

As in any of the other cases discussed above, be sure to confine the potty issues to the potty. Sometimes, these kids seem so 'bad' that parents start to dislike them and it flows out into other areas of life. Be sure to give lots of love and hugs and positive attention around the good things your child does. I know it can be tricky but you can do it.

I wouldn't use these words in any other area of parenting but this — the "child from hell" scenario   is about winning. You need to win this particular fight. It's about who's in charge, and it simply has got to be you. If your child is running the show, it's unsafe. When I say 'win,' I don't mean you should engage in a power struggle, but you should mean business. It most likely will not be easy, but it will be better in the long run for your child and the harmony of your home. The "new way" must be the absolute, and that means putting pee and poop in the potty.

So, to recap: if you're dealing with any of these scenarios, you'll need to go through the blocks of learning discussed in Chapter 5. Your child may breeze through or get stuck on some, but the process should give you a more organized sense of what went wrong and where. If you think you need a big breather to gain some fortitude, that is fine. In Chapter 16, I lay out the plan for re-diapering while you regroup. Every one of the groups of kids described above could do a reset, if you think you need one. Don't worry, a reset is not a step back. We need you in the right frame of mind. You are driving this particular car.

Chapter 12: Daycares and Other Caregivers

Okay — daycares can throw a major wrench in the potty training process. I used to believe that everything hinged on having your daycare on board. But in the last year, I've changed my mind a bit and have helped many, many parents negotiate success with or without the daycare's cooperation.

Before you even **begin** potty training, find out your daycare's policy. Most larger daycares will have a formal policy. Home daycares and nanny situations may not have a formal policy, but they'll still have their own opinion of how this should go down. So **find out**. Ask them many questions. Many daycares say they will work with you, but you'll find later that they really won't. Alternately, they may have some weird notions of what they can and can't do. It's best to find out what they do before you walk in on a Monday morning and are shocked. Some daycares are well versed in potty training and will help as much as they can. The bummer is that most aren't, so here's the un-sugar-coated version of what's going on.

Unfortunately, last year, the American Association of Pediatrics, in part sponsored by — oh shock! — big diaper companies, released a statement saying that the best way to potty train is to keep diapers **on** until the child is potty trained. We'll get to that particular insanity in a second.

Daycares gleefully took this policy on. Not having to deal with potty training is a huge load off their minds and hands. Potty training a large group of children isn't easy, I realize. Still, I want to point out the ludicrousness of this attitude.

How on Earth can you expect a child to learn a new behavior while actively engaging in the old behavior? Have you ever tried to get a kid to eat broccoli while he's munching on candy? Or let's say you want to cut down on TV watching. By this logic, you should keep the TV on until the child is ready to watch less. **This is nearly impossible,** and actually requires a huge amount of skill and thought from a **child**. It really, really makes my head almost explode.

The people who should be the most informed about child development are all just nodding their heads as if this new recommendation makes perfect sense. WTF?

So, back to daycares. What I've heard from many providers is they simply don't have the time to attend to a child with the speed necessary during potty training. In other words, they know that when a kid's gotta go, he's gotta go **now,** and they can't respond that fast. That's kind of messed up, don't you think? It makes me wonder how long these kids are sitting in dirty diapers.

What is more important than learning a life skill? Imagine if a daycare **offered** to potty train. Holy crap, they'd have a waiting list five years long and could charge double. What are they doing that's more important than that? Learning shapes and colors and dramatic play is all well and good, but learning to put pee and poop in the potty? Even better.

Daycares are essentially screwing you, especially if you are a full time working mom or dad. (Though I'm sure you're used to getting screwed by everything at this point, eh?) Because

immediately after daycare comes preschool, and guess what? Preschools demand absolute, full-on potty trained.

Ridiculous, yes? Yes. It ticks me off to no end. But the reality is I'm sure your daycare does care wonderfully for your child, and I'm sure you don't have much of a choice, so we'll deal with what we've got. I'll go through the best way to set you and your child up for success, and how to deal with the less ideal scenarios.

Take off as many as days in a row as possible to start potty training. Something like a three-day weekend with one extra day tacked on is usually great. I know this is not the ideal way to spend a precious vacation day, but it's worth it in the end. If you can take even more time off, that's great. If daycare is more a social thing and not a necessity, consider keeping your child home for a couple of extra days.

In that time frame, while potty training, **really** try to learn your child's pee pattern. Remember, that's how much and how often your child typically pees after "x" amount of fluid. The good news is most daycares have a sort of formal arrangement for snacks and such, so usually fluid intake is controlled. Still, you want to have an overall awareness so you can pass on the information.

As you are potty training, be sure you are saying to your child what you would like **him** to say. Remember when you were teaching "bye-bye," you probably very naturally said **his** words: "Bye-bye Grandma!" Right? Probably in a high squeaky voice too. And eventually he started saying, "Bye-bye."

Same thing with potty training. So as you are getting him to the potty you would say, "Mama, go potty," or "Mama, pee." Something along those lines. This is something that **all** parents should do, but it's especially important for you because, ideally, we need your child asking to pee as soon as possible when he returns to the daycare (realistically, though, self-initiation doesn't fully begin until one to three weeks after your start date).

Don't worry about the nap diaper at daycare. Send a diaper. It's a pretty useless fight that you probably won't win.

The commando issue is a big one that daycares resist. I think everyone is just weirded out by the idea of no underwear. I wouldn't even ask their opinion/permission if you can help it. Wearing underwear is simply too confusing for your child in the beginning. The snugness creates a muscle memory of a diaper and the covering suggests privacy. I can almost bet you that your child will have more accidents if you put undies on her too soon. Many schools will claim it's a sanitation thing/code/restriction/law. It's not. They are lying/pretending/scared. It's up to you how you want to play that. I've done the research. It's not a law or code. I've had moms do the research and it's not a law or code. But these people **are** in charge of your child for many hours. You don't want to be too contentious.

Let's say it's gone pretty well at home. Your child is getting it but isn't done by any means. The day you return to daycare, fill the teacher in. When you first get there, take your child to the bathroom and show her the ropes and anything particular to school. If the bathroom is not accessible to your child, ask to have a potty chair in the room. If they don't allow that, I'd seriously considering moving daycares. It's **imperative** that your child have access to the bathroom. Not just for ease but because ideally, we want your child doing this independently.

Tell your child clearly **who** is available to help him. Name names, point, have a discussion with the adult and your child. Daycare can get confusing and you want your child to be sure he knows who to ask for help, even if it seems totally obvious. In pointing out a source of help, scope out his favorite teacher. There's always a preferred staff at daycare. Look for the good cop, the sweet one, the patient one — find her (or him) and give directives to that one. Don't go to the meanie, if there is one.

It's perfectly fine if they take the children at set intervals. It's not how I potty train at home, but with groups of children, it works wonders. The herd mentality works in our favor here. They need to be taking the children at least once an hour, preferably every 30 minutes or so. I had a daycare tell me they didn't have the time except for once every 2 hours!!! That's too long (and kinda bullshit if you ask me).

If you know your child's pee-pee dance, let the care provider(s) know. Again, there are obvious classic dances, like hopping from foot to foot, but some kids get really quiet and some may get louder. Whatever your kid does, let the daycare know about it if you can.

Arrange a special signal between the teacher and your child. The best one is having your child tug on the teacher's arm.

I don't know why, but children sometimes get embarrassed about asking to go to the potty and drawing attention to themselves. You'd think pooping in your pants at the sand table would be at least equally embarrassing, but it's not. Go figure. Anyway, a non-verbal signal can nip this in the bud.

Ask the teacher to please save your child's spot whenever she goes to the bathroom. This is a big one. Many, many children are fearful of losing their spot and/or the toy they were playing with. Once they know they won't lose it, they are more likely to take potty breaks.

Make sure the teacher isn't staring them down while they try to use the potty. Every place has a different arrangement. If there's a stall and low toilets, the teacher can take your child to the bathroom and semi-close the door. If there's potty chairs in the room, great; just discourage hovering. I had a little girl, Emily, who was doing fine at home. However, at daycare, she would hold it and hold it and she would try to sit, but wouldn't pee. The teacher was getting sort of aggravated. After some questioning, it turns out she was hovering over Emily, pretty much demanding that something happen. It won't work that way. Once the teacher started being more casual and averting her own eyes, Emily did great!

Same deal as above for pooping. Pooping needs privacy.

Check out where the other kids are in the potty training process. If your child is the first one diving in, use that. Tell your child he's the first and he can show them all how to do it. If he's the last, use it. Tell him he wants to be a big kid like the other kids. If there are others at the same stage, use it. Tell him who else is doing this so he's not alone.

If daycares use a rewards system, it's fine. Just stay steady at home with no rewards. If you child asks for one at home, simply say, "Oh, no. That only happens at school, honey." In my experience, it's never been a problem or confusing. Not ideal, but the school has to deal with that potential treat-monster. The children I've worked with have never had an issue with things being different at home.

Those are all the big things. You don't want to overwhelm your daycare with a huge list of instructions. You should get a feel for how they are going to be with this by asking a few simple questions. A sample conversation might go something like this:

"Hi! We're going to start potty training Sally over the long weekend. We believe the best approach is to remove daytime diapers. We'd be delighted if you could help us in this process. How do you typically handle potty training? I'm sure you have vast experience. We'd like to combine forces with you for the most successful outcome for Sally.

Do you take the children who are potty training to the washroom at certain intervals? How often? How many accidents do you 'allow' before requesting a diaper be put on?

As long as Sally is showing progress I'm sure we can work on this together.

I really value you as Sally's care provider. We feel the timing is right for potty training. Anything we can do to assist you, please let us know."

In saying this, you've stated what you would like in no uncertain terms, you've done a fair amount of transparent ass-kissing, and you've stated how much you value the daycare. All good things.

You most likely will get a response like, "We'll work with you however you're doing it." Sounds great, but ask more questions! I've had so many parents gloss over this and end up with a nightmare.

I don't know why, but daycares can cop an attitude regarding who knows more about child development. They may say, "It won't happen till age three," or, "Children can only potty train in pull-ups." Somehow it becomes a little power struggle about who knows best. The best way is simply to state your desires for your child. A good daycare will do their best to work with you. What a daycare is not allowed to do is to re-diaper your child without your permission, unless there's an emergency, such as an episode of diarrhea.

Quick tangent: I potty trained Pascal at 22 months. He was at a lovely home daycare. The care-giver completely thought he was too young to potty train. Now, this might have been a cultural difference because she was fine with her 5-year-old drinking from a bottle. I told her he was doing great at home and we'd not had one single accident. She was appalled at his going commando. It was summer and she felt that when he was playing, everyone could see his penis. I was like, who cares? They're all under 2! She fought me on the nap diaper. I offered to bring in my own mattress and sheets for the crib. She refused. Anyway, it was a huge battle. I told her in no uncertain terms that he was not to be in a diaper. One day, I arrived there earlier than usual for pick up. He had a diaper on with his underwear over it! It was CRAZY. We switched daycares that day. Now, I live in a city that has many daycare options and I realize this is not true for everyone. Still, be aware that **a daycare provider is not allowed to go against your wishes**, as long as those wishes are clearly stated.

My advice is to really get a feel for your care-provider's attitude. You'll be able to tell, just by body language, tone and the words they choose, how they are going to act. Again, this is where some daycares get huffy about their authority.

Don't fight, but gently prod and fully express how you'd like potty training handled. Some daycares will pull out a policy, written down — 'cause that means it's real — that states your child must stay in diapers until potty trained. Gently try to work your way around this. The best way is to act **totally** stupid, like, "Gee...that's weird. I would think it'd be hard to learn something new while actively taking part in the old. Hmmm...that seems very odd."

If it's looking like they won't budge, that's okay too. As I stated at the beginning of this chapter, I used to think this was the end of the world. But it's not.

I used to write letters, on behalf of my clients, even talk to daycares on the phone. Moms would be getting ulcers trying to knock sense into them. And, yes, **we got our way**. But then we had daycare providers on edge — they were nervous wrecks, totally over-prompting and hovering. No good. We need this process to be stress-free for your child. An anxious provider is going to derail things even more than a diaper.

If your child **has** to wear a diaper at daycare, there's just not much you can do about it. What you **can** do is keep with the (diaper-free) system at home. Most parents figure out a way to make this work. It should look something like this:

Drop him off at daycare, go to the bathroom for a pee, put the diaper on him while in the bathroom. Tell him, "This is in case there's an accident. You should tug on Miss Suzy's arm when you have to go pee, or you can come by yourself." (if that's true). Say no more and no less. You're not letting him off the hook of potty training, you're not suggesting he just use the diaper to pee in. You are being vague on purpose. You are assuming he will use the diaper as underpants. It's a hard way to potty train, but it's do-able.

Same deal for pick up. Go to the bathroom for a last pee before the car ride home. Take off the diaper and leave it there (in the proper receptacle, of course). Tell him, "We're going home now and you don't use diapers at home. Remember to tell me when your are going to go pee."

What this does is to reinforce the notion that diapers are equated with daycare. It's a daycare thing and, oddly, this generally makes sense to the child. If the daycare is okay with changing diapers, so be it.

Having to do diapers at daycare is not preferable and it can make potty training drag out a bit, but not indefinitely. Still, having a stress-free environment (rather than fighting with daycare) is going to make this so much easier for all of you.

I have also found is that a little passive-aggressive behavior on your part never hurts. You can say something along the lines of, "Well, she's doing great at home but it's okay to wear a diaper here since you don't really handle potty training. I don't want you to be nervous." So yeah, act nice and slide the dig in. I understand if that's not your cup of tea but it does work.

I also find that daycares' attitudes depend upon what you tell them, so be sure to focus on all the success. If you walk into daycare and tell them it's been nothing but a struggle, that's exactly what they are going to see (and, I swear, partially create). If you go in telling them it's going great, they will feel the need to follow through with that. If it's going just okay at home, try not to say much of anything.

If your child is having very little success at home — and I mean very little — it's okay. Some kids do take longer to potty train than others. In such a situation, I'd be sure to check in with the daycare, honestly. Tell them you'd love to give it a shot at daycare without a diaper to see if she's just being obnoxious at home.

I know this is shocking, but our kids can be angels with other people and save all their crappy behavior for us, the parents. Enlist the daycare's help as a resource: "I know he's so good for you. We've done potty training this weekend and it's going...eh. Would you be willing to try today to see if he does well with you?" This usually gets a favorable response, again thanks to some transparent ass-kissing.

If your child is in daycare for a large portion of the day, you might want to consider day- and nighttime potty training, all together, at the same time. It can look overwhelming, so read the *Nighttime Training* chapter again and give it some thought. If daycare insists on a diaper and your child is there eight hours, five days a week, she's going to have very little time left in the day without a diaper on. Just something to consider.

So, in summary: **find out** the daycare's policy and/or how they handle potty training, with details. If they are willing and able, go for it. If they seem resistant, try to bring them to the light. If they are adamant about a diaper, call out their stupidity by acting really stupid yourself. If they insist on the diaper at daycare, proceed with potty training when your child is at home. If you need to fudge facts and act a little passive-aggressive, this is survival, baby — it's okay. (Hey... where else do you get this free pass?)

The bottom line is we can't hold off potty training until daycares get on board. You will miss the window of opportunity. You will also not have much time to wrap things up before preschool starts. You want to gently push the issue as much as possible, but it's completely do-able to potty train while your child is full- or part-time in daycare, even a resistant one.

Chapter 13: Behavior vs. Potty Training

This is probably the trickiest issue I address in this book —
separating out behavior from potty training. There is a lot for
your child to learn when potty training. Certainly the first few
days, and maybe even the first few weeks, are full of learning.
Learning, by nature, requires making some mistakes and/or
accidents. However, there is a difference between learning
and behavior. When your child is showing behavior — and I
mean of the bad variety — the behavior must be addressed.

First, I need to cover some ground about boundaries
and limits, then I'll hit specific behaviors I've seen in
potty training. Boundaries and limits have a bad rap in
parenting of late. They can seem mean or draconian or too
authoritarian. Many parents don't believe in any sort of
consequence or discipline. Let me state outright: I do not
recommend nor do I believe in hitting a child. Ever.

Chances are you are potty training somewhere around the
2-year mark, and around the same time, you may see some
other 2-year-old behavior. This may well be the very first
time you are seeing your child act up, but it's normal. The
terrible twos (and even threes) aren't just a cliche; they are
real. In normal development your child **must** test limits. It's
his job. He needs to find out where the fence is, so to speak.
The reason you physically fence in your yard is so your child
can't wander and get lost. Limits and boundaries are the
fence in your child's psyche. With them intact, just as in your
yard, your child feels safe and secure knowing where he can
and can't go.

A trend in modern parenting is to assume the child is capable of deciding good things for himself without being provided any boundaries or limits. This is just not the case. I often look to the Montessori system for examples of how to allow children to make decisions while also providing boundaries. Within a certain framework, the children are free to make choices, but they are not free to do whatever it is they want. Johnny might prefer Tinker Toys to Lincoln Logs; that's his freedom within that play center. But Johnny isn't allowed to wander aimlessly through all the toys. The children all eat lunch together. You can't have a bunch of kids with access to the snack fridge and leave it up to them to decide when they are hungry — you would have mayhem. The children all go outside together, whether one is tired or not. Our children require some fences. Within those fences we can allow for tremendous freedom.

Bringing Up Bebe by Pamela Druckerman was released to a torrent of mixed press. Ms. Druckerman claims that the French, in general, are doing a better job of parenting than Americans, largely because of the French notion of *cadre*. *Cadre*, loosely translated, means framework. French children are given a strict framework, but within that they have tremendous freedom. There is much I don't like in the book — or rather there's much about what the French supposedly do and don't do that I dislike — but I agree fully with *cadre*.

What I see, both in my life and in my work, is that a lot of us parents struggle with providing freedom within boundaries. In our quest to raise free-thinking, independent children we are not providing enough of a framework for them to feel safe.

I've mentioned *Simplicity Parenting* by Kim John Payne a couple of times. Mr. Payne was a Waldorf teacher and is so brilliant and eloquent on this topic, I can't recommend this book highly enough. He says that raising children is like building a pyramid. The widest part at the bottom is the foundation. That is made up of "governing," and takes place roughly from birth to age six. Next is the middle of the pyramid, made up of a "gardening" phase that takes place from roughly 6-12 years and last, at the top, is the "guiding" phase, which is the way he recommends parenting children ages 12-18. He suggests that most parents have flipped the pyramid and are trying to guide our children when they need governing. By govern, he means providing boundaries and limits, not cruel or harsh punishment. When a parent tries to guide a child whose frontal lobe — the part of the brain responsible for logic and reason — isn't fully formed, it backfires. Then that parent is left to govern when the child is older and should only need guiding. Now, from own personal experience, I see this in my own community. I see children raised with no limits or boundaries who, by the time they are 5 or 6, are wild and very hard to control. By this, I mean that they exhibit out-of-control behavior, not that they should be "controllable" like a puppet.

Payne also uses the analogy of you, the parent, driving a car. Imagine the anxiety your child would feel if you were driving, they were in the back seat and you had no idea where you were going. I've extrapolated that idea even further. Imagine if your child were **responsible for giving you the directions**, and that you just followed their directions. Go left. Go straight. No. Left. Wow. You'd soon be lost, yes? That's where things can get mucky with the oft touted 'child-led' model of parenting. You can be child-led in that you listen to and validate your child, but you simply cannot follow your child's lead through life. You both will get lost. The car you are driving is life, and it's your job to know where you are going. Ironically, many of the parents I've worked with and have known in my personal life are striving to give their child a 'free' childhood. Still, how free is your child if he is fully responsible for the direction the car is traveling? It's very anxiety-provoking. A truly free childhood should be about chocolate or vanilla, and little else.

All this is particularly true if you have a spirited or strong-willed child. I often work with parents who have a child fitting this description. This child is usually challenging in general, and will be challenging when it comes to potty training as well. Still, this child needs boundaries and limits just as much as, if not more than, your garden-variety kid.

All well and good, Jamie, but what does this have to do with potty training?

Well, sometimes behavior kicks up during potty training. And because potty training is so wrought with emotion, it becomes hard to pull it apart from behavior. I also find that parents will put up with all kinds of behavior during potty training that they wouldn't in other circumstances.

For example, one of the biggest challenges parents today face during potty training is getting their child to sit on the potty. Yes, you can read to them or sing to them. I say it's okay to play with a mobile device as a distraction in the very beginning. But really, when you ask your child to sit to go potty, your child should sit. Now, to a lot of people that sounds harsh. But if you take it out of the context of potty training, it sounds perfectly reasonable. Say it's time to sit down for dinner, and your child keeps bouncing up (assuming they aren't buckled to a chair of sorts). You tell your child to sit and they don't. How do you handle that?

I'm asking because — whatever your response — that's how you're going to handle it during potty training. When it's dinner time, it's time to sit and eat. When it's potty time, it's time to sit on the potty. Same thing.

Whenever you encounter behavior during potty training, do your best to put it into a different context. That will help you figure out how best to handle it in the context of potty training. It's totally your parenting call. I do not nor have I ever felt comfortable telling people how to handle behavior in general. That's why I'm giving you a framework to work within, and you can make your own parenting decisions.

Many parents say, "I don't feel comfortable making him sit." I agree. I don't think you should force your child to sit. However, it's worth pondering just how fearful we've become of transition to the potty. Many parents fear doing **anything** negative around potty training. Using a firm or stern voice sounds negative to these parents, and they're concerned about traumatizing the child. This is where another scenario comes in handy. Every single one of us has held our child down and strapped them into the car seat. Even when they are kicking, screaming and hitting. We do it because we must go somewhere and we need them to be safe. Has your child ever been traumatized by that and never wanted to sit in the car seat again? I'm guessing no. Again, I'm not saying you should force your child onto the potty or strap him down, or anything remotely like that. I'm just pointing out that this fear of traumatizing a child by conveying the message that you mean business has gotten a little bit out of control.

Another thing to keep in mind is the difference between "the child you have" and "the child you want."

—————————————— *From the Blog* ——————————————

The kid you have. This is a good one.

You have the kid you have, not necessarily the kid you want. This is especially true when potty training.

I can give you suggestions about any special circumstances you may have, but we cannot change your zebra's stripes. Still, this is hard for us to admit and hard to remember. We all want the well-behaved, loving, courteous child. We got what we got. Still, our love is fierce. While you are potty training, be careful not to linger in the land of "I wish he..." We can deal with what we have, but we cannot deal with a fantasy. Your kid comes with all his own crazy, his own stuff, his own DNA. There's a lot of nature in this here nurture. I encourage you to work with your child's strengths; while potty training, I'll never try to "fix" a weakness. We build on what your kid inherently has.

There's another aspect to "the kid you have." If your child has a particular "problem" — say he's whiny, or she's resistant, or prone to histrionics and tantrums — you are going to have this same kid when you are potty training. No judgment; there is no behavior I have not seen. Still, I see parents who somehow think potty training is going to happen in a bubble — that all the other behavior the child exhibits is somehow not going to appear while potty training. This is a big transition, so these behaviors will not only be there, but may even get magnified for a short period of time.

Again, it's all good. Just keep your expectations level and your love big.

I've worked with many parents who forget "the child they have," and really have an expectation that I can fix intrinsic behavior. I worked with a client, Denise, whose daughter Sienna was very strong-willed. After many, many conversations, Denise went off on me. She told me that she was not impressed with me or my method. She said I had claimed I could deal with "this behavior."

I cannot fix your child's general behavior. That's up to you.

Whatever you child's personality is, I can't change that or fix it; that's built in. If your child is exhibiting behavior you don't like or you feel is disrespectful, you will most likely see that very same behavior while potty training. What I *can* tell you is how to deal with some of the behaviors you find in potty training.

Here's a clear example of behavior. Say your child did great for a few days. Suddenly, she doesn't want to use the potty anymore. This can look like a defiant "NO!" or it can look like she just can't be bothered with it. If she sat and peed/pooped on the potty more than one time, then we know she can do it. Period. It's that simple. If she subsequently chooses not to, it's behavior.

If you're not sure whether you're dealing with behavior or not, look inside and see how you're feeling. If you are feeling sad or a little heartbroken that this isn't going as you intended, chances are your child needs more learning. If you feel like you are being played, if you feel angry, or if you feel like strangling your kid, I'll bet it's behavior. Most times, parents have a really good sense when they are dealing with behavior, but don't do anything because they are terrified of "traumatizing" the child. Having boundaries and following through is not going to traumatize your child, in any sense.

When you have a kid who you know is playing you, the absolute best thing to do is give a small, immediate, appropriate consequence. For instance, take away the toy he was playing with when he wet his pants, or take him out of the activity in which he was engaged. Time outs are usually not effective for "accidents," nor are longer-term things like saying he can't go to swim or dance class. If he has an accident in the morning, it doesn't work to threaten to take away dessert after dinner. Toddlers just don't have that extended a thought process. This is why sticker charts are useless. Toddlers don't have the thought process to say, "Wow. I have 6 stickers, 1 more and I'll have a week of staying dry!"

The small, immediate consequence is also helpful when you aren't sure whether he needs more learning or is exhibiting behavior. I think I've made it clear that pride and self-mastery should be the motivation behind potty training. However, for some children that never clicks in, and they need some external motivation to nudge things along. Some parents react along the lines of, "But I'll feel terrible if I give him a consequence and he needs more learning." Taking away a small toy as a consequence is not going to scar your child for life. And it's really the fastest way to get an answer. If your child can't use the potty knowing that his Thomas will get put on the fridge for an hour if he doesn't, you can bet your butt he needs more learning. And he won't be scarred. If you child **can** do it, then you know the accidents are due to behavior. I'm interested in real-world potty training, not theory. Consequences will get you your answer the fastest.

Some parents say, "Isn't a consequence just the opposite of a reward? I'd rather reward the behavior I want rather than give a consequence for what I don't want." I understand the theory behind this and yes, in general, positive reinforcement works best with children. However, we go back to that notion of **expected behavior**. The problem with rewards and potty training is that they get sticky. The stakes need to be raised constantly in order for them to be effective. If you are going to reward for peeing, where else will that lead? This, of course, is your parenting call. Personally, I would rather curb undesired behavior than reward the hell out of good behavior. Else, you end up with a kid who expects to be rewarded for everything.

My son started kindergarten last year. His school has a system of rewards, called Kennedy Kash. Basically, when you are "good," you get a Kennedy Kash, which you collect and can use to "buy" something at the school store. This is all based on positive reinforcement, you follow? If you are "bad," you don't get a consequence, they just amp up everyone else's Kennedy Kash. So now, my son gets this Kennedy Kash for breathing or paying attention. And the kids who are misbehaving have stopped caring about the damn Kennedy Kash, and still misbehave. It's a total disaster of a social experiment. I don't want my child getting rewards for breathing. Or paying attention. That's what I mean when I say that the stakes have to be raised constantly in order for a reward to be effective. You have to keep amping up the rewards. So no; a consequence is not just the opposite of a reward. I fully believe in rewards for exemplary behavior, and I also believe that bad behavior gets a consequence.

I add that I think you should differentiate between the child and the behavior. Your **child** is good and always will be. Her **behavior** is/can be bad. This is very important.

Moving on. If you are getting **overtly** defiant behavior — like your child is looking you in the eye and peeing on your carpet — this is different and is very serious. I discuss this further in the chapter called *Under 22 Months, Over 3*, as generally, this sort of defiance is found in kids over 3. Bottom line, it warrants serious help right now, because it is not about potty training — it is about anger. Deep anger. I highly suggest you contact a family therapist as soon as possible. Otherwise, it will only get worse and could escalate into potentially dangerous behavior.

Of course, once again, **you** know your child best. I just adore this post from a mom:

"So I modified your method a little (okay maybe a lot) because I know my son and we would have ended up with a fridge full of toys. I took the basic concept of what you said and did the "WHEN you do THIS I will do THAT." I said, matter of fact, "Let's go try to go pee pee on the toilet" and took his hand and he said, "Okay mommy."

We walked to the bathroom and I closed the door behind us and suggested we read a book. He said no and would not sit on his potty. So I said, "When you pee pee in the potty, we can go back to playing." When he realized we were going to be in the bathroom until he peed he SCREAMED for every toy/ video/treat he could think of.

As he named each one I said calmly, "When you pee pee in the toilet, we can [play with this or have that]." We went through the list one by one as he brought up each toy, and this lasted for almost 40 minutes. I read one of his books off to the side (trying to seem uninterested in whether he went or not) and suddenly, he sat down and peed on the toilet! An hour later, he did the potty dance and we went back to the bathroom again and had WAY less drama this time, I'd say it took less than 10 minutes and he didn't sit this time, he stood up and peed in his toilet! This morning was the same thing; I took him to the bathroom, closed the door and it took maybe 5 minutes before he peed in the toilet.

At daycare, when we first arrived, I walked him straight into the bathroom that is attached to his room. He smiled and happily pointed at everything and named it, "Toilet, sink, soap," and I said, "Yes, this is where you will pee pee today, and this is where you will wash your hands," etc...

We tried to go pee pee but he didn't go and I told him that was okay; we could try later. I followed your advice, didn't mention what a disaster it has been, and just told them that he does not say when he needs to go every time so it's best if you put him in front of the toilet about every hour. When the teacher took him in there the first time he didn't pee until they stepped out of the bathroom, so he had an accident in his pants. But after that he peed in the toilet every time today!!!!!!!

I feel like we turned a corner last night, and I know we have a ways to go until he learns to tell us before it's time, but I feel a huge weight has been lifted off my shoulders. THANK YOU!!!!!!!!!!!!!!!"

What I love about this mom is that she knew her kid really well. And while she took my general advice, she knew how to tweak it to make it work for her son. She knew he was being stubborn and she took it as a challenge — a good kind of challenge — and she was **right**! Once over that barrier of behavior, she was met with consistent success.

As I said, this is a tricky chapter. I'm an over-thinking, over-educated, over-parenter, as are most of my friends and clients. I know I've probably stated some things that have pushed your buttons. That's okay. This is how it all makes sense in my head as a mom and in my work as a potty-trainer. If something doesn't fully resonate, think about it, run it through a sieve in your mind, keep what makes sense to you, and ditch what doesn't. Most of what I've addressed here has to do with "parenting philosophy." My personal parenting technique is not to be tied to any one school of thought. Just as I suggest you do, I filter through things and keep what makes sense and ditch what doesn't. If your philosophy is no longer working for you, you can start to change things. I like to think of what I'm teaching in terms of whether it will work for the long haul. I'm not just raising a son, I'm raising a man. With that, here is one more article:

From the Blog

So I had one of those parenting moments last week. You start with this one dot and then you're connecting dots all over the place, and pretty soon, it's like your head's gonna explode.

It all started with Taking Down Christmas. Pascal absolutely made me promise that he could be a part of this and that I would not do it while he was at school. It is an all day project, what with the tree funeral and all. The Day To Take Down Christmas was January 7th. Had to be this day. There was no other day. All weekends coming up were spoken for.

January 7th arrived and here in Providence, RI, it was 62 degrees. Oh man. I felt that crazy pull — do I give up the chore of the day to go outside??? Now, I'm very active and so is Pascal. We like good weather. Plain, basic weather doesn't dictate our staying in or going out, but this seemed too rich to pass up. Still... the Christmas had to be Took Down. That Day. In the back of my head all I could hear was the SOCIETAL pull to Get out! Enjoy the weather! Long story short, we managed both, but it got me thinking (always a dangerous thing). Simultaneously, my social media news feed of choice was flooded with the sentiment:

"May your children look back on today and see a mom who had time to play. There will be years for cleaning and cooking but children grow up while you're not looking."

My inner WTF alarm started going off. My inner Sassy started talking back, "Well, when my kid is grown, my house will still be clean from the last time I cleaned it. And when my kid is grown, I won't be cooking nearly as much. I can go hours without eating. He can't go one."

My Inner Sassy got replaced by my Inner Pissed Off: "Okay. Current media message: family dinners are the most important family ritual to have! Eating out is unhealthy! Processed food is unhealthy! You must make everything from scratch! Including the nut-free, soy-free, dairy-free, gluten-free, sugar-free cupcakes for the whole class!"

Add that to the not-so-breaking news: "Helicopter moms are ruining kids! The first generation of kids who were raised by over-parenters have hit the work force. They are entitled and praise seeking without putting forth any real effort."

Declutter! Organize! Both HUGE new business models and blog topics.

So riddle me this, Bat Man. When the hell am I supposed to keep my house so orderly and clean and have these amazing meals on the table if I'm dropping everything to play with my kid?

More importantly, what am I teaching my kid by dropping everything to play with him?

Are we supposed to be entertaining our children? Or raising them to be a one in a whole community?

First off, these simple platitudes piss me off. They raise an impossible, invisible bar on us as mothers. You know what they do? They make you feel like you are screwing things up. That you are not good enough. That if you do more, you'll be better. I have always hated the platitude, "Live everyday as though it were your last." I get it. I'm a full liver-of-life. However, if I were truly going out tomorrow, I wouldn't really care if your kid were potty trained. I get the sentiment but, c'mon, already.

But let's say for minute that we buy into the platitude. (And I think some people are buying into the platitude. I even think some people think this makes them a better parent.) Again, I ask: what exactly are we teaching here?

Are we teaching that our world revolves around only them? 'Cause I'm not sure that's the best thing.

My son knows in a thousand ways that he is my heart, walking around outside my body. I smother him in smooches, snuggles and I love you's. We have a rule in my house that when he says "Will you read to me?" everything does get dropped and oddly, this has never been abused. Am I really supposed to be down on the floor playing with him?

What happened to, Go Play? Are we somehow terrified that our kid won't know we love him? Or are we micro managing? Or does it make us feel good, like we're doing something ACTIVE, thus showing we are indeed, PARENTING?

If you consistently drop everything for your child, isn't that what he comes to learn? And to EXPECT from others? Are we teaching our children they must be entertained and stimulated every second?

Or are we afraid of the inevitable, "I'm boooored"? Boredom is good! Boredom begets creativity. Boredom gives birth to sticks becoming wands and tree forts, castles. Real, honest pretend rarely happens when a grown up is lurking about.

Don't get me wrong. I'm ALL about impromptu breaks in routine. But isn't a diet of all entertainment a bit like a diet of all candy? Isn't downtime good? And aren't daily chores teaching life skills?

Still, I'm looking around me and seeing parents who are taking this too far. Decluttering and organizing are INDEED booming businesses, because many kids (that turn into adults) aren't being taught the value of organization. I'm meeting unhealthy 20ish people who don't know how to roast a chicken and steam vegetables. I'm meeting people for whom finding clothes and getting dressed in the morning is a struggle. We ALL know plenty of men who wouldn't know HOW to clean a toilet even if they could RECOGNIZE when it needed cleaning.

Now, I'm a single mom with a 5-year-old. My home and life have to be in order. I can not afford to get behind the eight ball. Ever. I like my affairs in order because having things hanging over my head feels like low-level anxiety and I don't like that. That makes me a decidedly not-good mom.

But here's my take on it, in general. I'm not raising a son. I'm raising a man — someone who will one day be a loving and gentle PARTNER in a relationship. Someone who will be one of a whole community and value his place there. I think cooking and cleaning CAN be fun for a kid, and educational to boot. I think keeping a clean and organized home is essential to a child's well being. It provides the structure by which to have fun. Just this morning, we got our first snow. We were able to go outside, play in it, come in, read a few books and play a board game...all BEFORE school. This is largely due to the fact that our home is organized. Meals are planned. And yes, the fact that we arise at Oh Dark Hundred gives us extra time. When the work is done with rhythm and routine, there's really even more time for the fun.

I don't think I'm all that. This is what works best for my family.

Chapter 14: EC

This chapter is for you if you've used Elimination Communication (EC) in any form. It doesn't really matter how long you've ECed or how consistently. I want to personally say thank you for saving us all (x) amount of landfill space! I am currently working with Andrea Olsen of *GoDiaperFree*. We both are well aware of the huge gaps in bridging EC and potty training. We are constantly working with each other to find the most effective way for you to move from one to the other. While we toss our ideas back and forth, I will share everything I know about getting from EC to potty trained. Some of what I have to say is probably going to raise your ire at first. I ask you to please read and absorb with an open mind. I've worked extensively with ECers and this is what I've found to be true. I have no interest in arguing. My only interest is getting your child to pee and poop on the potty. I'm going to hit the main points I've personally run into with clients. If some of this doesn't apply, just disregard.

Most of my former ECers come to me when their kids are somewhere between 16 and 24 months. I've heard of some EC kids who are not yet potty trained at 36 months and beyond. I'm not sure what to think about that.

Now, you're reading this, which means regardless of current EC literature, you know in your heart it's time for completion. I'm going to call this completion process a 'bridge' for brevity; a bridge from there to here.

I initially contacted Andrea because I was getting more and more clients who wanted potty train before 20 months. I fully support this but found myself "warning" people this would be a certain percentage of ECing and a certain percentage of PTing. But then I realized, holy crap, I'd **heard** of EC but I certainly didn't know all the ins and outs. So enter Andrea. Of course, I think it's brilliant to have avoided as many diapers as possible in your child's life. However, there are some things that are part of EC that will make PTing a bit difficult.

1. Diaper Free Time
2. Catching the pee, not moving physically to the potty
3. Philosophy
4. The idea that your child will just potty themselves.
5. The expectation that EC gives you a jump on PTing.
6. Potty strike

Diaper free time: You are probably already aware of this, but Diaper Free Time has most likely conditioned your child to pee on the floor. This particular practice almost made my head blow off when I heard of it. I talked to many in the diaperfree.org association. Apparently this practice is used to teach cause and effect, which is an okay theory but not that great in reality. I remember when I was pregnant reading a brilliant article about toddlers. The gist was that toddlers aren't really out to bug the hell out of you or kill themselves. There's just **so** much to discover that every moment is an experiment and discovery. So when they pour their milk out onto the floor, it's for the joy of seeing, "Oh..**this** happens when I do **that**. Cool." And yes, that is cause and effect.

However, it's our job as parents to let them know that pouring milk out onto the floor is not acceptable. While we wouldn't yell or shame them, we would consistently probably frown and say something akin to, "No, no...no milk stays on the table." Right?

So, now let's look at the cause and effect of peeing anywhere, anytime the urge hits. If you never let on that it's unacceptable...then it's acceptable. It's therefore learned behavior to just pee where you need to pee. This might be okay in the early days, regardless of what age you started ECing but once your child consistently does this for any big chunk of time, it's sort of cemented in. In other words, you've traded in a diaper for your floor.

The only reason I bring up Diaper Free Time is because the very first thing I hear from an EC Mama is resistance to a naked day. When I first met Jean, the first thing out of her mouth was a kind of angry, "I do **not** see the point in a naked day. I have done months of naked days and all I do is clean up pee". I still have to ask you to do the naked day. The naked day is vitally important to one of the biggest steps in building the bridge from EC to PT, which brings us to issue number two.

Catching the pee: Thus far in EC, you probably have an amazing bond with your child. You know her signals and you rush to potty her, mostly where it's convenient. I LOVE the fact that EC gives you "permission" to potty anywhere. However, once you officially start potty training, you do want to get your child to the potty of choice (either the little potty or the insert on the toilet). The big thing here is getting the child physically to the proper place. Every potty training mom has had to get her creative pee catching groove on in a tight spot. But the norm has to be getting the child to the potty. I'd say this step alone is the biggest in the bridge from there to here.

Philosophy: I know "traditional potty training" is a dirty phrase in EC. I know there are "boot camps" for potty training and all kinds of coercive methods or advice. I hope by now, you realize I'm very pro-child and feel very protective of children. However, at certain times I find myself having to remind parents that it's okay to have boundaries and expectations. There's a lot of philosophy around EC and attachment parenting that sometimes falls apart as your child nears the "twos". I don't think the twos need to be terrible by any stretch, but you may find that some of this EC-associated philosophy doesn't hold up. I don't want to argue this point and I'm not saying anything about anyone's parenting style. I simply find this is a hard place in parenting to maintain theory. Your child will begin limit testing and his favorite word will likely be "No".

A lot of the philosophy out there suggests that there can be nothing negative around the potty. Much as in the milk on the floor cause and effect example from above, you do have to tell your child what your positive expectation is and what the negative expectation is. This does not have to sound mean but you do need to mean to be business. At some point your child must learn that peeing just anywhere is a "don't." What I find is a lot of parents emphasize the positive end of things (only pee in the potty), but they leave out the other part of the equation (don't pee anywhere else). So, yes, you definitely want to stress the positive, but make sure you are being clear about what you **don't** want as well.

The expectation that the child will potty themselves: Once in a while a child will decide to potty themselves. Usually this is not the case, however, which makes sense if you think about it. And that's probably why you are here. Peeing and pooping are primal behaviors, right? You don't have to teach a kid how to pee or poop. Putting it in a **container** of some sort is a socialized behavior. Socialized behavior must be taught. If I want something you are holding, the most effective way to get it is to slap it out of your hand. That is primal. The socialized way of getting it is to ask or negotiate. **That** is what must be taught.

How do we teach that? When our children use the primal instinct to slap something out of someone's hand, we look them in the eye, we say in a pretty stern voice, "No hitting. You ask." We probably frown or make a disapproving facial expression. We are more effective when we use simple language. NO this, YES that. There doesn't need to be a ton of talking about it. I think all of us, as a whole, are doing way much talking. I especially think this is true in potty training. It's similar to your child learning the ABCs. They aren't learning all the power behind the letters that make different sounds at different times in millions of combinations. They just like the song. In potty training, the short, more direct words work best.

The really hard part: Now the hardest part, I think, about bridging EC to PT is dealing with the expectation that because you've been working at it for a fairly long time, this should be easy for your child. Believe me. I think this should be true as well. I don't want you to be mad at me but what I've found is this isn't necessarily the case. It's a real fucking bummer. You have worked hard and deserve a jump on potty training. And the fact that you're probably not going to get one is really hard to wrap your head around. What I **have** found is that once you're over the hump, ECed kids tend to move much faster and the training 'sticks' much more. And you have the bonus of not only a great bond but also of **knowing** your child's signals.

What I've found works best for ECers who want to potty train is to simply think of this as another (separate) process. Your child probably hasn't made the connection that she is the one who should be in action once the feeling of having to pee strikes. And your child is probably very used to peeing as the urge hits, wherever that may be. These two little connections are the biggest.

Making these connections is not hard physically. This is a turn around in your head. It's the slightest adjustment that will make this so much easier. When I met Gwen I think we went around her philosophy for days. She didn't want to say anything negative about the potty. She didn't want to do naked day. She really thought her 22-month-old daughter would, any day, turn around and potty herself. I pointed out that Gwen had come to me, so clearly she thought she needed help in her daughter's completion. She did, indeed... but she had such a hard time, thinking all her work of ECing was going to waste.

In fact, she was pissed at EC. If a child can be potty trained in under a week, why'd she waste all this time trying to help her child connect the dots with EC? Maybe you're feeling something similar. I know a lot of people do. I encouraged Gwen to think of all the positives. Not clogging the planet with crappy diapers, having an incredible bond with her daughter. Mostly, the greatest thing is that she already knew her daughter's signals. This is incredibly hard for some moms who've diapered to figure out. They haven't kept 'track,' so to speak, and they are starting from ground zero. From diaper moms I almost always hear, "She didn't show any sign she was going to pee." Now, you, as an ECer, know better. So you do have some advantages.

Another pitfall is when your child is taking longer than average. I had one former client, Jill, who flipped her lid. On 'my clock' she was on her 4th day of potty training. But because she had basically done Diaper Free Time for 6 months, she felt like she'd been potty training for 6 months and 4 days. So it was very frustrating to her. She kept yelling, "I've been at this for months!!! When is it going to be over???" And I kept saying, "We're on the 4th day of potty training!" We had to really look at it like EC was wonderful and then it stopped and then potty training began and it was its own process. Once she made peace with this is, it eased everything up for her.

Potty strike: A lot of moms write in that at some point their child started arching and resisting the process. I actually think **that** is the signal to start in with potty training. In PT, almost all resistance is caused by us being too focused on the process. By hovering and over prompting. I really think this is the reason for the resistance in EC. You have been catching pee for a long time and it's all you are probably thinking about. All my ECers come to me with pee logs. Ditch them. You don't need a pee log. You know your child. I really do believe when you edge off the process and start prompting them to go on their own, they will step up.

Differences in the actual day to day PTing: So, I encourage you to do the first few days as I've laid out here. It's really just that physically moving your child to the potty when they are mid pee. That's the most important step.

The only real difference if you've been ECing is that you don't put away the potty you've had out. I only recommend doing that for people who put the potty out for the child to get used to it. Most often it's misused as a toy. Clearly, in your home, it's been used correctly.

Should your child pee on the floor, clearly and firmly state that is not where pee goes. Pee goes in the potty. Other than that, those first few days should be done as explained.

I sincerely commend you on your ECing. I'm thrilled to be able to help you with teaching your child to completion. It's okay to have many feelings about me, EC and all I've said. I know many, many moms who are really upset with how little EC addresses the reality of completion. And I know many moms who were upset with me when I presented them 'my case.' My intention is not to upset but to pave the smoothest road to potty training as possible.

Chapter 15: Younger than 20 Months, Older than 3 Years

We could also call this chapter, "PTing outside of my time frame."

I always recommend starting potty training between 20 and 30 months. In my vast experience, that's where the magical window of opportunity lies. Of course, many people want to potty train before 20 months and some parents, for whatever reason, have waited until after 30 months.

If you are potty training before or after my suggested time frame it's still doable, but there are certain considerations of which you need to be aware.

Under 20 months

It is completely possible to potty train under 20 months. A few things that might come up for you are:

Lack of communication: I've discussed this elsewhere but it's worth mentioning again. Think about this: your child is constantly communicating with you. It's up to you to decipher. Your child most likely is at the 'point and scream' stage. While this is a delightful way to communicate it's not always effective when potty training. The best thing to do is to teach your child the sign for pee...this can be Standard American Sign Language or it can be made up. However, I suggest a vocal cue because often times you aren't looking right at your child. The word Pee is easy enough. Some moms have used other vocals or can recognize particular screams. One mom figured out her daughter made a specific clicking noise. It became their signal for 'gotta go.' I would not worry about differentiating between pee and poop as far as words. It's going to come soon enough.

Pulling down the pants and physically manipulating clothes: I copied this blog post in an early chapter but it's worth reading again:

─────────────── *From the Blog* ───────────────

Yay! More and more parents are choosing to ditch the diapers at around 18-20 months. For most kids, it's so easy at this age. BUT a lot of kids don't yet know how to manipulate their clothing. Nothing is more frustrating to you OR your child than knowing they have to pee, making the move to the pot only to be tied up with mangled attempts to get THE PANTS DOWN. Ahhhhh!

So a few things can help. First off...who the heck started saying PULL your pants down? Toddlers are very literal.

While teaching them how to use their pants, use the words "PUSH your pants down." That's really what they're doing, right?

Definitely, start having your child dress themselves. This in and of itself is huge. It gives them SUCH empowerment! And some massive skill building. When you are teaching your child to dress themselves, it can sometimes require a few more words than, "I'm putting your pants on". Remember:

this is a brand new skill to them! So really break down what you are doing: "I'm hooking my thumb into the elastic, see? And then I can GRAB them and PUSH them down."

Some parents have found a "dressing" party has helped. Much as in playing with dress-up clothes, spend an hour trying on outfits. Make it seem fun! Practice is the key here and most kids at this age don't get a whole lot of practice. And the pressure of a pee looming doesn't make for the best learning, either. So set up some teaching time to literally and figuratively get the pants down.

And some of you may think I'm a whack job and way over-thinking things. But I can't tell you how frustrating it is to be THIS CLOSE to consistent pee in the potty and have the damn pants mess you up!

Prompting: Your child is going to need you more than an older child would. You will prompt on those easy catches I refer to in that all important *Prompting* post. You must keep in mind that **you** will be responsible for your child peeing more than the parent of a 2-year-old would be. Your child **will** get it and **will** eventually initiate but they will need more help.

On that note, while potty training, teach your child to get you for help: Charlene, a mom I just recently worked with, figured out her 19-month-old would say 'up.'

Charlene thought she wanted to get up in her arms. She was half right. Her daughter wanted up to be carried to the potty. It only took Charlene two times of being peed on before she figured it out.

A little potty chair is essential: Baby Bjorn makes a great one. Companies that specialize in EC gear have very small potties available. These should be easy for your child to either sit on or back themselves onto. It's pretty vital to have a little chair available. I often get some version of this: "We don't really like the little potty chair. We prefer he learn right on the big toilet, since that's where he'll be going." That's okay, I guess but my question is, "Don't you want him to be able to go on his own?"

Until your child can physically manoeuvre onto the big toilet, he's going to need your help. I think it's well worth the $20 to get the little potty. Soon enough, he'll move to the big toilet. But if he has the notion to go on his own, we certainly want to make it available for him to do so.

Be aware that this is much more of process for the younger child: I don't mean that it's harder, I mean that it can take longer. Progress can be slower **and that's okay**. Just don't expect it to be done in week. I find that to be pretty rare. The thing to look for is progress, not perfection. As long as you see him making consistent progress, it's all good.

Be really ready to tell everyone to frick off: No. I'm serious. If you know in your gut that your kid is capable of this and you feel ready, **go for it**. But society is going to tell you up, down and side-wise that you are crazy. I do not think this is so. I congratulate you on your intuition! Fabulous. Rock on, Mama, and don't look back.

You will start the plan just as I laid it out in Chapter 5. Always remember that the goal is to move along the timeline from **Clueless** to **I Peed** to **I'm Peeing** to **I Have to go Pee**. Each little component may take a bit of time. It's all good as long as you feel progress.

I hesitate to even mention what I'm about to, but it must be mentioned. The child under 20 months can be 'not getting it' for a while before it clicks. You can still potty train a young child who is a little clueless, but it will take longer and it's really going to be on you. If you work outside of the home and don't have a willing care provider, you should probably wait. I would say overall, a month is a very realistic time frame for progressing through the timeline. Does a month sound too long to you? Then wait. If that sounds amazing — one small month to be done with diapers — proceed.

I've told this story three other times in this book, but I'll tell it again. My first attempt at training Pascal was at 18 months. At the time, I was single mom (still am), I owned a clothing store and his daycare was very unwilling (thought he was much too young). Within a day of potty training, I knew he wasn't clicking on his own. I was bummed because I knew it was possible for him, but in my life, at that time, it would have brought more stress. I let it go and he potty trained in a matter of days when he was 22 months.

You don't know what kind of potty trainer you have till you jump in and go for it. At this age, if it's not going according to plan you can always re-diaper and it will not hurt the process one bit. There is a lot going on developmentally before 20 months and they just may not have the skill set. If you feel able to be there and help, that's awesome. I'm not trying to scare you or be a big bummer but I want to be realistic with you.

Potty training the child over 30 months.

If your child is over 30 months but under 36 months, you're heading for a danger zone but you are not fully in it yet. There's hope. The very first thing a mom with a kid over 30 months will tell me is "I feel so guilty. I waited too long and now the window of opportunity is gone."

First off: ditch the guilt right now. Leave it on the ground and walk over it. Guilt serves no one. I'm sure you honestly thought you were waiting for readiness or the right time. I'm really sure you didn't think, "Wow. I'd really like to fuck up potty training." So leave the guilt. You are where you are and that's okay.

You are going to do the training just as I lay it out in Chapter 5. The only thing you need to really be aware of is the behavior stuff. The resistance that comes from a kid over 30 months isn't usually because of learning. It's usually just because you are saying one thing and they are automatically going to say another. You are definitely going to dance between prompting and the backing off. The older child needs much more privacy, so pay close attention to that. They also need much more independence. The 'walk away' prompt is the best. That's when you remind them in a casual

way, such as, "I can see you have to pee. There's your potty."
And physically and mentally walk away.

The older child is also going to most likely have poop
troubles. Go back and read all the *Poop* chapter, paying close
attention to the "glaring spotlight." These older kids are just
that much more attached to the security blanket of diapers.
Privacy and independence are your best bet. As I've said, 30-
36 months is not a danger zone...just sort of a no man's land
of fuzziness. It's time to really do this now, with conviction
and consistency.

If your child is 36 months or over...

We don't have time to beat around the bush. To me, this is
the danger zone. I know many people are convinced that 3
is the new age to potty train. In my experience, it's infinitely
harder.

So again, ditch the guilt. You are where you are and we can't
change that. Okay? I'm imagining you were 'waiting till she
was ready' and now she's showing no signs of being ready.
Or you need to get into a preschool. Or something clicked in
your head to get this done now.

Whatever the case, it's seriously time to put your big Mama
panties on and really get this done. When a child is 3 or
older, there's actually very little learning to be done with
regard to the potty. It's highly unlikely that your child is
brand new to potty training. Most kids at this age have
simply rejected your attempts, be it in a big, violent tantrum
kind of way or a constant peeing-in-pants quieter way.
Regardless of what you've done in the past with your child,

go ahead and start the whole process as I lay out in Chapter 5. Even if you have some success under your belt.

Former client Mary came to me because her son, Dillon, was 38 months. He was being denied admission to a preschool because he wasn't fully toilet trained. Dillon could pee on the potty most of the time, but poop was hit or miss. Sometimes he'd do it in his pants, sometimes make it to the potty. He was still having a few pee accidents as well. Sometimes he was wildly resistant to the potty and other times, he'd just go. It looked like a hot mess and of course, Mary was going crazy because of the preschool thing. It was, like, **serious**.

I recommended she go back to that first naked day. She really fought me. She didn't think he needed to go back. She felt that he had made enough progress that he didn't need to go backwards.

But in a case like this and maybe in yours, **we need to know where it went wrong**. You can't go back and fix something if you don't know what went wrong in the first place. Right? And clearly, something went wrong. It's about going back and getting those blocks of learning, those phases, rock solid. And playing around with them if they are not.

In short, Mary went back and did the progression of blocks like I laid out. And it clicked for Dillon. We never did get an "ah-ha!" as to what went wrong. It wasn't very clear to either of us. But just going back and doing it all in order, made it work for Dillon.

The best analogy I can make is say a kid has learned 20 letters of the alphabet. That's a good chunk of the alphabet, right? But kind of useless without the other six letters. Now, you can't just throw those letters at the kid and expect him to put them in order. You have to start at A and then go to B and insert the letters into the alphabet. I know and you know that he's got A and B but without going back over them, the kid will have no frame of reference with regard to the other six letters.

Same thing with whatever struggles you are having with potty training. I don't know what went wrong and I'm guessing you don't know what went wrong. So just start over. The parts he's got will just be review. And as with Mary, I wouldn't look for some big "ah-ha!". I've done this with thousands of kids. I know, know, know this progression works.

So that's your first task. Take it back to the beginning. While you might not have an "ah-ha!" moment, it may become very clear that you were over-prompting and not handing it over to him enough, or something similar. The biggest problems I see in kids over 3 are behavior issues. My party line is that most kids start to hit individuation around this time. This is the psychological process by which your child starts to separate from you. This age is marked by pushing against you and limit-testing. It's good and normal but when you add pee and poop to this you've set yourself up for the granddaddy of all power struggles. As I'm sure you know. I'm not saying that to rub your nose in it — it's just good to know what you are up against.

The best way to end a power struggle is to let go of your end of the rope. All right, Jamie...so how the eff do I do that?

You give this (responsibility for the learning) to them. You don't argue. You don't cajole. You don't beg or negotiate. And you never, ever let them smell your fear.

You begin that first day with, "We have not done a good job with potty training, so I'm going to help you learn it the right way. You're going to help by letting me know when you have to pee or by going yourself. There's the little potty or the big toilet. You can choose." Most kids are really waiting for you to show up with the consistency. I'm not saying that's always the case, but often it is. So here you are, waiting for them and all this time, they've been waiting on you. I know...fuuuck. It's okay, though.

If, during that day, you are met with resistance, you continue to back off. For instance, use that throw away prompt of, "You have to pee, there's your potty." **You must leave room for him to make the good decision himself**. This could take a day or two, so be patient. You want to dance along the delicate line between prompting and backing off.

Now, for most parents, that's going to be enough. Time after time, I've seen moms shocked at how quickly and easily it went with a former Potty Monster. Often, I really think it's a matter of a) the consistency and b) going back and learning. If a kid doesn't "get" all the components of a process (like potty training), they tend to stop caring. I call it the "inner fuck it." Which is basically them saying, "I suck at this, so I'm not going to try." Our kids **want** to do well. They **want** to do the right thing. We have to believe that. A lot of resistance in the older kid is because they haven't learned something quite the right way.

You see this same attitude coming from the kid who's kind of the punk in school. He slouches, doesn't pay attention, is the class clown. It's usually this kid who, it turns out, never learned to read or has a learning disorder. We want to assume your child is just missing a component.

Now you might start at the beginning, make it through a few days, and everything seems ok. Then you go back to daily life and whoops...poop in the pants again. I highly suggest using a small, immediate consequence. **Not** as punishment, but more to find out if your child can use the potty properly if motivated to do so. We need to know if this is them not caring or being lazy about it or if this is something they can't control. It becomes very clear whether or not they can do what we're asking when we add in an external motivator. The consequence should be something that matters to your child but nothing overboard. As I said, this is a pretty quick, non-invasive way of figuring out if your struggles are due to behavior or something else.

It's helpful to separate out potty training from behavior. If your child **won't** sit when you ask him, that's behavior. If you know your child **can** use the potty because he's done so in the past, though at other times he can't be bothered, that's behavior. Behavior always needs a consequence. Often, clients tell me that it sounds wrong to give a consequence when dealing with elimination issues. What I like to do (as

I've recommended in a previous chapter), and I encourage you to do as well, is to put the behavior into another context. If you child doesn't want to eat to dinner and he takes his plate and dumps it on the floor, what do you do? An older child who cannot be bothered to sit and put his poop on the potty is doing just that. "Nah. I'm good. I'll just poop in my pants and you can clean it up."

It's been my experience that you can **feel** when you need to use a consequence. You will feel like a game is being played and you are the sucker. You will feel like you are being 'abused.'

Now, if you are still having accidents but it doesn't **feel** like behavior, here's the most recent deal: many, many children — especially kids over 3 — are actually constipated. **Listen up:** this can be true even if your child is pooping 3 times a day. There can be backed up poop and it could be creating difficulties across the board. I know how crazy this sounds, but it's true. What many parents have learned is the easiest way to figure this out is to get an x-ray done. Your doctor will be able to tell you. Your doctor might also recommend a prescription laxative. This is by far the most common protocol. I certainly don't want to alarm you but this situation is becoming more and more common and I'm not sure why.

The biggest marker for potential constipation is that your child is over 3 and sincerely seems to be trying — I mean over an extended period of time, not a few days of potty training — and they show remorse at accidents. They seem to honestly try to make it but sometimes the poop comes too fast. Or whether they make it to the potty in time seems completely random. What I've come to learn is this sort of counterintuitive constipation really messes with a child's ability to feel the poop is coming. If you have a little one over the age of 3 who does seem to be trying and can't get the poop in the potty consistently, I feel like an x-ray is a pretty easy fix before things get worse. There is also a program called *Soiling Solutions* for children over three and a half. I hear wonderful things about this program, so though I haven't personally used it, I feel very confident in recommending it.

But there is another variety of the older child that gets ugly. This is the child who is being resistant in an "eff you' kind of way. This child will look right at you while he's peeing on the floor. You will know if you have this variety. It will **feel** aggressive and you will feel hostage to your child. This behavior needs to be addressed head on. This is not funny and can lead to serious issues later on. You must deal with this as behavior, and behavior only. Do whatever you would do as if he looked you right in the eye and said, "Eff you." Cause that's kind of what he's doing. I highly suggest contacting a family therapist if this is happening. This actually is not at all about potty training. I do think it's serious and I do think you should seek help and not take it lightly.

Bottom line: when you have a child over 3, potty training needs to be addressed in a very straight-forward manner. It needs to be done, and done now, at almost any cost. The child over 3 is much more likely to have bigger problems. I know so many parents are fearful of seeming 'hardcore' —

they don't want to traumatize their kid. I get that, totally. I never want to see a kid traumatized, either. But in my humble opinion, getting kicked out of kindergarten for potty training issues is a lot more traumatizing than being super strict now.

Chapter 16: The Reset

I've coined the term 'Reset' for those instances in which, for whatever reason, potty training has completely unravelled and you need a do-over. An erase. A start again.

The Reset can be used only once. It is NO GOOD if used more than once. It means you re-diaper your child and forgo all things potty and potty training. The optimal length of a Reset is 2-4 weeks. Any shorter isn't enough time and any longer can create more "addiction" to the diaper.

The best way to tell if you need a Reset is if you are at the end of your rope. By this, I don't mean you're feeling the normal exhaustion and frustration that the first few days of potty training can bring. Rather, the Reset is for those of you that have given it your all, and I do mean your **all**. I want your child potty trained, yes. But I also want you sane and your home harmonious. If you are feeling strung out, a little insane, and you've been cleaning pee off the floor for more than two weeks, consider a Reset. If your entire life revolves around trying to figure out when this kid is gonna let loose and you have no other thoughts besides potty training, consider a Reset.

There are two major times to do a Reset.

1. **Before using this book:** You have tried potty training in any way, shape or form and you have a disaster on your hands. Or even just a hot mess. So you heard from a friend about my book and you ran to the computer to buy it. You are gung-ho to start but you have this writhing mess on your hands. RESET.

2. **After getting this book and giving a really solid effort:** Either your child never got it or got it and her behavior suddenly flipped and she's crazy every time you mention the potty. Also looks like a hot mess and you cannot figure out what happened. RESET.

The Reset should never be used with a child over 3. If you refer to Chapter 15, you will see that any child over 3 who's 'not getting it' is most likely showing **behavior**, not a glitch in learning.

The reasoning behind the Reset is this: first and foremost it gives you and your household a big breather. We need you sane to be effective. If you are crying over potty training, there's just no way you are going to able to keep firm and consistent. You **will** slip into bribery and negotiation. I know this. Much like a torturer, your toddler **will** break you. And you'll be all over the map, which sends the signal that you are not in control. If you are not in control, your child is. And that's unsafe for your child.

The other thing the Reset does is it gives your child a chance to collect himself with a status quo he knows (diapers). Potty training is a lot to learn. But if he is resisting you, he is stuck in a rut. Much as during a tantrum, nothing can be learned from this place (you ever try to reason with a tantrum-ing toddler? Yeah...right?). If your child is stuck in a rut, there's really no point in continuing. The days where there are fights are not days that count toward good potty training. Nothing was learned.

Finally, the Reset lets your toddler "win" a little bit, which is a good thing. It can settle her and make the next go-around calmer. She won one, you get to win one. I know that sounds odd, but it's true.

As a side note, perhaps you are not getting resistance, just utter cluelessness from your child, and wonder whether a Reset is warranted. In such a case, you have to be the judge. Utter cluelessness for more than a week is something I have never seen in a child over 24 months of age. I've seen kids not want to deal with the potty or pretend it doesn't exist, but that's not cluelessness. That's passive resistance and should be worked through. We'll talk about kids younger than 24 months in a minute.

So how do you handle a Reset?

First, you re-diaper. I'd prefer you do this at night before bed and just continue doing so in the morning. The one thing I'd like you to avoid is returning to diapers in the middle of a fit of resistance. She's screaming and you say, "Fine! Put a diaper on!" This is her "winning" (in a very different way than the good kind of "winning" I mentioned a few paragraphs ago), and it will send the wrong message.

The message we want to send — and you can use these exact words — is, "You are not using the potty properly, so we are going to use a diaper again so we can all calm down." This isn't meant as punishment or giving in. This is merely to regroup.

Second, you put away the potty chair and you don't say boo about potty training. You will mostly likely get one of the following reactions:

1) Nothing. No mention of it and actually you can sense relief in your child.

2) Your child asks about it but doesn't ask to use it. Use that statement above and then change the subject. This is not the time to lecture about her misuse of the potty.

3) Your child suddenly, for the first time, asks to use the potty. I'll get to this one in another minute.

Third, you breathe normally for the first time in a long time. You most likely will have the experience of "having your kid back." Enjoy this time. Don't linger in the past or be freaked out by the future. It is what it is and it's meant to be a time of regrouping and regaining harmony.

Fourth, set a new date. Again, 2-4 weeks from the start of the Reset is best. Your child will be marinating all the potty thoughts in her head. It won't all go out the window, I promise you. Hold that date in your thoughts and you can even throw it out there casually a few times: "You are not using the potty properly, so we put it away. Don't worry, we'll start again on Monday (or whatever)." Casually. Just so your child knows it's coming but it's not this looming fear.

Now, if your child asks to use the potty and it does seem like she will use it correctly, you can give her **one shot**. You can either take the potty out or you can use the insert. If she does indeed use the potty the right way, you can tell her "Thank you. I will leave the potty out for you. If you don't use it, it goes away again for a while." If there is even one time of her not using it properly, you need to follow through with the Reset. No matter what she says. This **cannot** become a game. It's either use the potty or don't use the potty. Again, if it becomes a game, it puts her in charge and that's not psychologically safe.

A few words about the Reset and the child' age. As I've mentioned, if your child is over 3, you will not want to use the Reset. Period. However, if your child is under 22 months, you may want to do a Reset but you will go about it differently. For the child under 22 months, there is a very real possibility that she is clueless. There's a lot going on developmentally and the timing may just be off. Please don't use this as a cop out. I have 16-month-olds who potty train with no problem. If you want to potty train between 16 and 22 months, that is awesome. Chances are your child has shown some indication that this is possible. Go with your intuition. You should have a sense of progress. If you see **no** progress, consider a Reset.

For this child, you do not need to put the potty away. If they indicate that they'd like to use the potty, it's fine. With this age, there's usually little to no behavior going on. The child is just really not connecting the dots. You still want to set a new start date, perhaps a little longer out than 4 weeks, for when you'll try again. You do want to keep that in your head, so diapers don't sort of take over.

Just to be clear, from 22-24 months is an unclear zone :). Sometimes a child can be truly clueless and sometimes not. It's for you to call. I would look back on their other milestones and see if they were on target or early or late. That's usually the best indicator.

Two things often happen when parents read this chapter or feel they might need a Reset. The first is that I'll hear from a parent who's at the end of her rope on the second day of potty training and wants to know if a Reset is appropriate. I'm very sorry and I don't mean to sound hard core but that's a ridiculously small amount of time in which to lose your marbles. Your child is learning a new skill, and no other major milestone has been achieved in so short a time frame. Put your big girl panties on and step up to the plate. This is your child and **you** have the magic. Adjust, get creative, think about what might be going on. There's a fair amount of thinking on your feet about your particular child that is needed here. Here I go again saying the same thing, but you are the expert on your kid.

The second reaction I get is massive resistance to the Reset — an overwhelming sense of, "**No way.**" The parents feel that the Reset would be a massive backslide. Many parents will point to the one pee they got in the potty in the last three days. "She did it once! See?" To which I say, "Listen. I truly believe in most instances that working through the problems is the best way to potty train. But one pee on the potty in three days in week two of potty training is not progress. You are stuck. The only way to get unstuck is to change something."

There's a great Einstein quote: "The definition of insanity is doing the same thing over and over again, expecting different results."

Chances are, by the time you are considering a Reset, you have tried many, many different things. For whatever reason, it's not working. We will never know why. But we do need to shake things up a bit, and that's what the Reset does. It shakes things up and also calms them down. While you are figuring out what might have gone wrong or what you could change, and at the same time you are still potty training and are getting nothing but pee on the floor, you are going to go insane. Insane moms are wildly ineffective teachers.

As I mentioned in the beginning of the chapter, the Reset is good for before or after starting this book. NOT BOTH. So let's say, you have a child who's 28 months. You've given potty training a pretty good attempt, not using my book, and now...you don't have a potty trained kid, per se, but you don't have a disaster either. You bought my book to seal the deal. If you don't have a disaster, I'd jump right in with that first day. Many times I hear, "I think she was just waiting for me to throw away the diapers." OR you can choose a start date in 2 weeks and re-diaper her till then.

If you have read this book because you **do** have a disaster, I'd definitely Reset your child before beginning again.

Once again, as throughout this whole book, it's impossible for me to know your exact situation. I trust your intuition and you should do the same. You know your child best. Weigh your options and see what feels right to you.

The Reset really, really is only good one time. Otherwise, you will teach your child that if they pitch a big enough fit, you will cave in to what they want. I think we can all agree that this is a disaster in the making.

Chapter 17: Special Circumstances

Extreme fear of the potty: As I mentioned in the *Drama* and *Dilemmas* chapters, you may have a child who shows extreme fear of the potty. This child is **rare**. I've only had 11 of them in all my years of doing this. But they do exist.

First, you need to ascertain that this truly is fear — not resistance, and not the usual minor fear a child will show at doing something new. One mom equated the appearance of "true fear" with that of a cat being stuffed into a small bucket of water. If your child looks something like that, the fear is real and it's there from the get go. Most often it appears that these kids are afraid of the actual potty, but it could also be the sensation of releasing the pee/poop or both. Sometimes it's unclear which of these two (or both) is the culprit. There's no talking to this child, and this isn't behavior.

The number one thing to remember is that this child will be able to learn **nothing** as long as she's in this place of fear, so don't even bother. If it looks like you have a truly fearful child (and you will know for sure within a couple of days) then I want you to approach potty training differently. You are going to go about it much slower and, contrary to all I've said elsewhere in the book, you're going to take a casual approach.

Casual potty training **is** possible. What happens in most cases, though, is that the diapers sort of take over and pretty soon you're not doing **any** sort of potty training. If your child is deeply fearful you have to go slower, but you will still be potty training. First, though, we must get past the fear.

You will keep the potty chair out, preferably in the bathroom, and it should be something like the Baby Bjorn chair. I'd prefer it not be one that can be used as a step stool or could be mistaken for anything but a potty chair. Take your child with you as often as possible when you yourself go. She can sit on it, with pants on, if she will. You can casually ask her if she wants to use it. Asking is okay with this child. You actually **do** need her permission. This is the rare instance of a child who does need to get used the potty chair. You can try to get her to pee on it before a bath or when she's getting dressed in the morning. You will move slowly. If she says no, you should say, "Okay. Maybe tomorrow." Keep at it, not like a pitbull, but with steady strokes.

Now, I've only had 11 kids to work through this with, so I can't claim to be a full-blown expert on the this kind of fear. But moving steadily at the child's pace worked perfectly for those 11. All took around 2 months of steady work, and then they were potty trained. I would venture to say that if the fear persists and you see no forward movement, look to see if there is another source of anxiety. More and more children are getting anxiety disorder diagnoses. If you feel your child is overly anxious, you should seek help. I'm not trying to freak you out but early intervention is by far the best cure. As I stated in the *Poop* chapter, I think the general state of the world is causing this anxiety in our children, not you or anything you are doing.

Preemies: If your child was premature by more than 4 weeks, spent any significant time in the NICU, or had trouble bonding, potty training could be delayed. However, this is not necessarily so, and by 'delayed' I mean it might come closer to 30 months than 20 months. I'm not saying to wait till she's 3-and-a-half. Preemies tend to be slightly behind their peers in other areas as well. I would look at other milestones. If all were a bit delayed, I'd factor that in to potty training. Do this not as an excuse to wait too long, but to give your child the time she needs to 'catch up.' Most kids I've worked with in this category are all caught up by 24 months.

Adoption: If you have adopted a child, particularly from another country, you should focus on forming a bond before beginning potty training. I once had a mom attend my class and it turns out that her adopted daughter came to her quite bruised. Due to lack of staff, the orphanage would tie the children to the potty until they had produced. Obviously, this child did not need to start potty training any time soon. I have never seen an adopted child have any problems with potty training, so I wouldn't give it any thought except to say not to rush it. If you adopted your child at a very young age, you can proceed with training as I've described with no problem.

When I first met Mona, she had just adopted her son who was 20 months. He was very bright and seemed very capable and ready to potty train. We both suspected potty training had already been started in his native country. He didn't click and after a few days started to show fear around the potty. We both decided that, given the huge transition he'd just been through, it would be best to go about training as I described above in the *Extreme Fear* section. Within a month, he was potty trained. Mona was thrilled because even though it took longer than she originally hoped, it was still pretty awesome to have him trained. It's almost the nature of adoption that your child, upon coming home to you, his Mom, is coming to a much better place. Regardless, this is still a **major** transition, as is potty training. Go with your gut and your motherly intuition.

Emotional and developmental delays: If your child has diagnosed emotional or developmental delays, then potty training could be delayed. I say "diagnosed" because every child develops differently, and while you may think something is up, it doesn't have to mean she's delayed. I know kids who haven't said a word until they were 3 and then busted out with full conversations. I sometimes see parents use this as an excuse: "Well, he's not really delayed but he doesn't do such and such...I don't know if he's ready to potty train." So I "require" a diagnosis in order to justify delayed potty training. Obviously, the severity of the delay will dictate when potty training should begin. This is best discussed with your pediatrician. I would simply ask, "Is there any reason Johnny can't start potty training?" For example, if the delay is just in language, there's no reason he couldn't. But if the delay is in processing information then things may not bode well for potty training until a little later on.

Just because your child is delayed doesn't mean you have to forgo potty training. These special circumstance kids make me think of an episode of *Super Nanny* (my not-so-secret indulgence). This episode featured a 5-year-old boy with Type 1 diabetes. This kid was a tyrant, completely running the house. He got away with anything and everything because his parents were so fearful of him dying. Super Nanny came in and a) showed them a list of successful people who lived with Type 1 diabetes and b) showed them how their fear was getting in the way of good parenting and setting appropriate boundaries. Once the parents started putting their foot down, this kid's behavior not only improved, but he was also relieved that he was being treated normally. It made him less afraid that he was going to die.

No matter what is going on, your child deserves a healthy and normal childhood. And the best way to create this is to do what you would do if your child didn't have whatever diagnosis he carries. So don't necessarily use anything as an excuse not to potty train. Again, it's best to discuss your particular situation with your pediatrician and see what limitations may affect your child. Be wary, however. My experience is that regardless of what the delay might be, children do best the earlier you begin potty training. You may be advised to pick your battles, which is fair. But potty training often gets put on the back burner, and then you have a 5-year-old in diapers. The reality is that yes, you are going to make sure your child has the proper speech therapy or occupational therapy. But don't just let potty training go by the way side. It will get harder with each year.

Megan came to me because she has two boys with Sensory Processing Disorder. This is a tricky diagnosis, just by nature. Her older boy started potty training at 3 years old. It took about a year for him to potty train, which seemed normal given the diagnosis. She had a gut feeling to try potty training her younger at 24 months, even though supposedly, he'd have the same difficulties. He didn't. He had some issues with needing to take all his clothes off to poop...but she didn't mind. She was thrilled that it took so much less time. She credited me for the success, but I don't think it was me. I think it was that she started it at the right time.

Whatever your child's diagnosis, again, look to their other milestones to get a sense of their learning curve. Children with autism tend to really hate transitions — all transitions. Potty training is one of the big ones. You can go about it the same way as you would for an extremely fearful child, if that seems to better suit your child.

Regressions & major transitions: We discussed regressions a bit in Chapter 3, but the subject warrants a little more. Remember, regressions are backward steps. In potty training, this means your accident-free child suddenly starts having lots of them. Most often, you hear about regression when a family is expecting a second child but really, any major transition can cause a regression.

With any major transition, especially a new baby in the house, of course your toddler wants attention. Most kids act out in some way with the new baby. If not through potty training regression, it's through hitting or biting, being mean to, or simply ignoring the new baby. This baby is getting cuddled and loved and held and can do no wrong. Your toddler is being told, "No, Don't, Stop." It's absolutely inevitable — you're giving your new baby more physical attention, simply because you have to. A new baby is helpless and demands it. So your toddler lets some of his big boy skills slip. Remember: negative attention is better than no attention in a child's mind.

How you address the older sibling's need for more attention is up to you. Many parents carve out special time for the toddler. I personally recommend telling him as often as you can how much you love both (all) of your children. That may seem obvious, but it's shocking how often we think our children know that we love them. They still need to be told. And they need to be told that your heart has enough room for everyone in your family.

I also recommend really playing up what your older child can do and the baby can't: "Wow! I can't believe you can ride a tricycle. Man, your baby sister is not even **close** to riding a big bike like that!" Or, "Wow. It's so great that you can pee on the potty and your sister has to wear baby diapers. I bet she'll be happy when **she** can pee on the pot. Let's show her how you do it, so she can learn from you."

Beware: this is to get you through the regression phase. You don't want to foster constant competition between siblings. You do want your child to know he's appreciated for his big kid skills and give him a one up on this new, cute intruder. Pride goes a long way in potty training.

REMEMBER: It's not just the new baby and the attention thing that can cause a regression. The whole family dynamic has been usurped. There used to be 3 people and now there are 4. Schedules are mixed up. Everything in your toddler's world has changed, even if outwardly it looks the same (which is highly unlikely).

I maintain that kids are like gas tanks. They run on empty sometimes. And when there's a new baby in the house, just about everyone is running on empty. But here's the thing: it really doesn't take much to fill them up again. I'm constantly amazed at this in my own parenting. Over a few days, Pascal will start nudging towards 'off' behavior — a little needy, a little whiny, a little cranky — just...blech. And then I'll realize I haven't really sat down and played with him or given him one-on-one time recently. When I do, the behavior goes away. Like instantly. Our kids don't need a bunch of our attention, but they do need it focused. Playing *Candyland* or *Uno* or even giving all your focus to building the damn *Thomas* track. Again.

Everything we do as parents, we do for our children. Our daily lives revolve around them, literally. So we think, "How much more attention could I possibly give this child? " I also think that it sometimes feels as though if we give them a little, they're gonna glom onto us and never let us go. In reality they need precious little. But it does need to be good, solid time. Oh crap, here we go with the infamous '90s and "quality time over quantity," but it's true. When I sit and play a game of *Uno* — and I mean sit and play *Uno*, no checking phones or emails or anything else — Pascal's attention tank gets full. Presto magic, all the wonky behavior disappears and he's off playing by himself again. I'm always amazed. So, don't carve out some faux time because that's what you've read about. Play something solid and fill up your toddler's tank. It will make it that much more understandable to him when you have to sit and nurse the baby.

While regressions may happen, it's not a given that they will. I've found that when you expect something to happen, it usually does. Don't let a fear of regression stop you from potty training your older child now, if you're currently expecting number two. To delay potty training is not going to be useful. A skill that has been learned and dropped is easy to pick up again. It will be a lot easier to regroup and get back on track should your toddler experience a regression than it would be to start from the beginning. It's like working out. Once you get in shape and get into a workout routine, even when you fall off the wagon for a while, it's always easier the next time around. You know what it takes and your muscles remember. It's better to potty train your child before another child is born. He'll get back on track **much** quicker than if you were starting from scratch.

Another point I want to make is that I have never personally seen a huge regression. Most kids have a few accidents here and there, but it's tough to gauge if that's from acting out or simply that the parents' attention is focused on the baby and not on prompting.

Yet another thing really worth mentioning: if you are pregnant right now and trying to decide if you should potty train before or after the baby, maybe nobody told you this, but one kid plus one kid= like 5 kids. You will not be coming up for air for at least 2 months after the new baby is born. You may not believe me but I'm telling you right now. Don't entertain the notion that you will be able to start potty training 2 weeks after the baby is born. It will not happen. Normally, a mom will come to me around 7 months pregnant. She'll have a 24-month-old and will be vacillating about whether she should start now or after the baby. In favor of starting now: she's got 2 months to seal the deal. But if she waits, that's 2 months until the baby comes, and then another 2 months to come up for air. And then another 2 months before she really feels semi-normal again. Realistically, we're looking at potty training at 30 months with a 4-month-old on her hands. Believe me when I tell you: shoot for potty training **before** the new baby. If you miss that window of opportunity, everything will be that much harder.

Other major transitions can also cause regression. Moving and divorce are two of the big ones. These situations are very stressful no matter what kind of game face you have on. Don't underestimate your child. She feels your stress. She absolutely feels the tension in the house, even if you think you don't say or do anything to express that stress or tension. Children are remarkably intuitive. They live and breathe by our energy.

Stress and tension may be unavoidable and I think it's best to say things out loud in terms they can understand. "You know, Mommy and Daddy are having a hard time right now. Can you feel it? But it's okay. We're going to figure out how to do what's best for our family." Alternately, "You know, I'm really nervous about moving. Are you? And I've been so busy packing and getting ready, maybe I haven't been spending enough time with you. Let's play something."

Don't bring up the regression during these conversations. Your child will leap to the conclusion that his accidents are **causing** the issue. Your goal is talk about the big, pink elephant in the house, not the symptoms you're all experiencing.

Listen to your child! This is an opportunity to let your child express her feelings. Once you open the door, you'll be amazed at what children will say. Just giving big topics attention will resolve a lot of accidents and other forms of acting out. Be careful, however, to not make promises you can't keep. Talk and ask questions, even if it feels like they are too young to understand. The information's getting in, you can be sure.

One final thought on regressions: do not put a diaper back on your child! I know this is the billionth time I've said this, but it's that important. Once potty trained, even in the beginning stages, putting a diaper on your child says one thing and one thing only: "I don't trust you. I'm telling you all day how I know you can do it and I have confidence in you. But really, I don't trust you." This is extremely damaging to the whole process. If you don't trust your child, they will never trust themselves.

And for the billionth time as well: your energy, your vibe, your non-verbal cues are leading the show here. Be sure and be steady.

Chapter 18: My Final Answers

Final answers. These are answers to the questions I get asked over and over. In theory, there are no stupid questions but in reality...well...

Basically, all the answers below are concepts that are fully explained in this book but, I'm often asked again anyway, so here are my unadulterated sassy final answers.

Do I really need a little potty?

> This is of course, your call. However, my final answer: YES. If you want to foster independence, you will need a little potty. It also creates a better squat for easy elimination. Most parents who try to go without one end up at Target at midnight after the first day of potty training to buy one. It's just easier to start off with one.

Can't I just try underwear? I'm afraid of...

> My final answer: YES. You can always try underwear. If you have some notion in your head that commando is weird or creepy, go inward and investigate that. I have heard some people are afraid of infection. I have never, ever seen this happen. I don't recommend panties in at least the first two weeks. If you want to try them, that's up to you. You have been warned. If the panties get soaked, don't be attached to them; ditch them.

Can you convince me he's ready?

My final answer: NO. I wrote this book. I've heard it makes sense. I cannot convince you that your child is ready. My final answer is that if **you** doubt it, it will look like a hot mess. If you are unsure, your child will be unsure. If she is unsure, you will be cleaning up a lot of pee.

Can't I try rewards? They worked for my neighbor/friend/ sister...

My final answer: This is up to you. I don't care how you do this. I cannot help you clean up the mess the rewards create. If you end up in a huge power struggle, that's on you to fix. It's not just a potty training issue. I see full-blown disasters **on top** of potty training nightmares because of rewards. You think you want to try, go for it. I have warned you.

I already started PTing with rewards. How do I stop?

My final answer: Just stop. You can explain it to your child or you can just say, "Nope. We don't do that anymore. Mom and Dad go pee and poop in the toilet. This is what people do. We don't give rewards anymore."

I can not wake up in the middle of the night for night training. What can I do?

My final answer: Buy more diapers. I don't mean to sound hardcore. No...I do mean to sound hardcore. I really have nothing to say about this. If you know you are absolutely not in the head/physical space to night train, don't. Wait until you are. But you are going to have to attend to it.

I don't feel comfortable giving a consequence for behavior around potty training. What else can I do?

My final answer: Not much. If you've ascertained that you are indeed dealing with behavior and not learning, you have to do something (please do be sure that the child doesn't just need more learning time). I'm assuming you are looking at a consequence because you feel like you've tried everything. Again, a consequence can be useful for figuring out if the child is capable. There's a lot of confusion about consequences. I'm not suggesting you come down on your kid like they burned down your house. I mean take away a match box car. It doesn't have to be done meanly or with a lot of drama. The idea here is to help teach cause and effect. If you have **no** consequence/discipline procedure in place (outside of potty training), it's time to put some thought into it.

Many parents, even friends of mine, think consequences for the potty are unnecessary for a 2-year-old and think it's "wrong" to give them. I'm here to tell you the truth: your 2-year-old will become a 5-year-old. And you can't waltz in with consequences/discipline for the first time when your child is 5. You can try, but it's hard. I have two friends that I had to "divorce" because they never believed in any form of discipline or consequences. They now have **maniacs** for 5-year-olds, with very out-of-control behavior. Just warning you. Again, discipline does not have to be mean. It means having a boundary and following through.

Our house set up is really poorly and the bathroom is far away...what can I do?

My final answer: Move. I'm kind of kidding, kind of not. That's up to you to figure out. I can't change your house. You can have small potties all around the house or even plastic party cups in every room. Get creative. But it's your house.

I feel like my child is really ready but everyone is really coming down on me to not do this. I don't want to push him.

My final answer: Fuck everyone. **You** are your child's mother. **You** are the expert. If you feel in your gut that your child is ready to potty train you should not let anyone tell you any different. You should also not post on Facebook about it. I can't give you the courage. You have to find that yourself. I trust you and your gut. That's it.

I only have about 4 days to do this and then we are traveling all summer long. But if I wait, I'm afraid I'll miss the window of opportunity.

My final answer: If you child is going to be 3 or over during this time frame, you need to take a break from travel and do this. Now. If your child is under 30 months, I suggest waiting. Four days is not nearly long enough to have this under their belt. I get many versions of this question. Again...I can't change your schedule for you. I can tell you this is a process. The more under pressure you are to get it down, the bigger a failure you will have. You will unwittingly put too much pressure on your child and it will not go well.

My child HATES being naked. What else can I do?

My final answer: Your child needs to be, at the very least, bottomless. You will not catch the pees unless you can see them starting. By the time the moisture is through the fabric, your child will be empty and the lesson will be lost.

It's freezing here in (...). Does he HAVE to be naked?

My final answer: See above. Jack up your heat for a day or two.

We're living at my in-laws and I don't want any pee on the floor...

My final answer: When you take off the diaper, accidents are bound to happen. I cannot guarantee that no pee will end up on the floor. You will also be prone to freak out if some does, which will derail potty training. I cannot change your situation for you. You may have to wait until you have other living arrangements.

My kid HAS to have his bottle of milk before bed. He will pitch a huge fit if he doesn't, what can I do?

My final answer: You are the boss in your house. Ditch the bottle. Unless you are brushing his teeth right after the bottle, you are contributing to your child's tooth decay. Yes, even with milk. If you still want to keep this practice, go for it. Night training will be hard. Your child will not be able to hold his pee that long. Of course, that's my experience. Maybe yours can hold it. Only way to find out is to do it.

Sorry if my sass bothers you, but it's intentional. I can't change situations for you and I can't just wave a magic wand (boy! do I wish I could). You have to be creative and use your judgement if your situation or your child isn't the "norm." Everything can be worked around if you examine it from all angles.

Chapter 19: Random Tips and Questions

Tips for the process

These are things I've found over the years to be tremendously helpful. Overall, go with what works and be prepared to fend off unwanted advice.

- Have stuffed animals, dolls, cars, trains or any other favorite toy "watch" your child use the potty. This works great the first few weeks. Kids love the idea of showing off to an audience of inanimate objects. It also works great for the child who doesn't want to leave an activity behind. The thrill of the "audience" seems to have limited power, though. Its magic fades after about a month or so (or whenever your kid gets hip to your shenanigans).

- Always offer choices — this works well in **all** areas of parenting. Do you want to use the big pot or the little pot? Do you want to go before Daddy or after Daddy? First, this gives the child some control, which they love. Second, it automatically implies that whatever you're asking them to do **is** going to happen. But within those boundaries, it gives the child some control. And third, it slips in some learning about the concepts of "before" and "after," and what they mean. Giving a choice works well as a prompt: "Come, it's time to pee — do you want to go first or second?" Giving choices is a great parenting trick in general, and can smooth other difficult areas, like getting your child to get dressed. Generally speaking, you should offer two options. Too many becomes confusing.

- Have a "poop book" or two, which are books you keep by the potty or toilet and read only while pooping. They don't necessarily have to be about poop. There are two reasons for this. First, it helps with the 'read every book in the house' problem. Second, it acts as a "prompt" along the lines of a nighttime CD. [Note: If you don't already use a nighttime CD to help encourage sleep, you might want to start. Select only one or two CDs to play at bedtime and **only** at bedtime, and soon, the music becomes a cue for sleep. In a short amount of time, your child will fall asleep within the first couple of songs. It won't work if you use the same CD to dance around to during the day.] Along those same lines — repetition and consistency — a poop book becomes a cue to poop, and soon, your child will poop within the first couple of pages. I'm serious. It's wild how well this works.

An added benefit is that pooping can require some concentration, and introducing new books at potty time will put your child's focus on the book instead of the poop, while a familiar book will keep the focus where it needs to bc. Then, too, you'll probably have the poop book memorized in short order, and will be able to recite it for your child when using bathrooms outside your home.

While the book doesn't have to necessarily be about poop, *Everybody Poops* and anything that combines Elmo with the toilet seem to be kid favorites. Ditto for Elmo on any videos about poop. I personally don't think you need any kiddie-potty videos but if you can stand them, have at it.

Elmo = toddler crack. But I'm not telling you anything you don't already know.

- Respect privacy. As potty training progresses, your child will request more and more privacy. Even in the beginning phases, however, while you do have to be present, don't get all up in your child's business. Don't keep looking between her legs or lifting her butt to see if anything is happening. You can be right beside her to assist or read without being focused on the action. Sometimes it even helps to look away or whistle, like you have no idea what's happening.

- Make it a habit to show or tell your child where the bathroom is in any new setting, including stores. Something simple, like, "Oh, we're in Target now. You know they have a bathroom over there in the back. Just let me know when you need to use it." When relevant, specify who, if anyone, is available to help. This is great for when you have a play date at someone else's home. Kids get confused — they may know you are a grown-up, but may not know that Pascal's mom is also a grown-up who can help. The "status" of teenagers can also be confusing to kids. If you are around teenagers who are willing and able to help your child, you can point them out. This is important because accidents tend to happen more frequently outside of the home due to reduced vigilance on your part and more distractions. Sometimes your time frame for getting to the potty is reduced dramatically when you're not at home.

- Be prepared when you're going someplace exciting. Toy stores, carousels, train stations — anything that thrills your child — will most likely bring on a pee and possibly a poop. Remember: the anus is a sphincter muscle that opens with emotion.

- To promote healthy pooping, be sure your child is adequately hydrated. Encourage drinking water over milk or juice. It's better for you and creates a great habit. Be conscious you're not withholding liquids as a way to try to manage accidents.

- Be creative and think on your feet. What works today, might not tomorrow. Come up with something new. If you come up with a unique solution that works for you but you've never heard of anyone else doing it, go for it! Every child, and every circumstance, is different. Go with the flow. I remember a former client, Diane, who was having a hard time getting her son Luke to pee in the potty. Luke loved everything about toilet paper. In a moment of insight, when she knew he had to pee, she put a square of toilet paper in the potty. Luke peed in it! THAT'S the kind of thing I'm talking about. A lot of parents get very nervous and want to do everything 'by the book,' literally. It's okay to use your own creative ideas if they strike. Just about everything is okay if the pee is landing in the potty and you're not doing anything too weird. I'll leave what constitutes "weird" to your own family parameters.

- Let it go! I know all this probably seems overwhelming. Don't worry. It's a lot of information that will become second nature in a short amount of time. You and your child will find your groove. Give your child the gift of responsibility, and back off. There's a fine line between watching your child and hovering; learn the difference.

Additional Issues

Teething: Beware the 2-year molars. If your child suddenly starts having accidents, it could be she's teething. Teething the 2 year molars, based upon my own observation, is hell. While all sorts of pre-teething goes on, when the teeth actually break the surface of the gums is the worst for your child. It can bring fevers, diarrhea and really "off" behavior. Do whatever it is you do to manage the pain, and do your best to maintain the status quo.

Getting sick a couple of days into potty training:
It's bizarre how often a kid will get sick a day or two into potty training. If it's a minor cold or is otherwise bearable in general, try to muddle through and expect to just stay afloat. If the sickness is not minor and your child is lethargic or bed-bound, it's okay to re-diaper and start fresh when he is himself again. He won't learn anything while he's sick anyway, so it almost doesn't count. Under these circumstances, re-diapering doesn't damage the process at all. Most kids seem to recognize that they aren't capable when they're ill. We also want your child focused on resting and healing, not learning.

Travel in the early stages of potty training: Many people have to travel soon into potty training, or live in remote areas where it's a long way to go grocery shopping. Depending on how your child is doing — and you will have a good sense of this about a week in — you have a few options. You could put a piddle pad (also called Chux) down in the car seat. These are big plastic squares with an absorbent middle — think disposable diaper spread out thin. It's also perfectly acceptable to use a "travel diaper." I would actually call it that so your child understands it's out of the norm — it's a "just in case." If you choose to use a travel diaper, put it on last minute before leaving, and take it off immediately upon arrival. You should also try your hardest to honor any pee calls even if your child is wearing the diaper. The travel diaper is especially useful for long plane rides. This is because traveling with a toddler is stressful enough, never mind have to keep a keen eye on the potty situation. Everything — but everything — is better when Mama's stress level is kept hovering around sane.

Hiring out the potty training: Don't be afraid to enlist help. I had a mom take my class and then I ran into her a month later. I asked her how it went and she said, "Fantastic. I hired my babysitter to do it. My daughter is totally potty trained." Hire it out if you want to! Most times this works extremely well because others aren't nearly as invested as we the parents are. There's no shame in getting help.

Swim diapers: These are fine in the early stages of potty training. The circumstances around swimming are special enough that using them doesn't create confusion, and won't derail the process. What will derail the process is having your child be the one who poops in the pool, and everyone has to get out, and all eyes are on you...and not in a good way.

Just put the diaper on your child at the same time as the swimsuit. Be sure to get a pee before getting in to the pool and upon getting out.

The same goes for the beach and lake. Use your judgement, though. If you have a beach house and are spending 8 hours a day on the beach, you don't want her in a swim diaper the whole time. You should encourage your child to get out of the water if she feels the need to pee or poop. And you should honor this request as if there weren't a diaper on. I know it can be inconvenient, but you are not using a diaper for convenience. You are using it so a big glaring accident doesn't ruin your life for a day.

My pediatrician said to wait till she's ready: I have some pediatricians among my clients. In fact, a few years back, when a few pediatricians used my services, they asked to make copies of my book for their waiting rooms. It's kind of how my book got on the map, really. When I switched my son's pediatrician and filled out all the registration paperwork, she noticed my email at *Oh Crap Potty Training,* and asked me about it. Then she asked for cards and brochures, saying, "I would love to have someone to direct my patients to! I don't potty train kids."

This makes perfect sense. Over the years, I've had innumerable clients tell me they tried to discuss potty troubles with their doctor and the doctor cut them off with, "Oh, just wait till they're ready"...which is fine, unless you **know** your kid is capable and just need some suggestions on how to get started or fix a problem you've encountered.

Here's the deal, straight up, no BS: Always listen to your doctor. But doctors get paid to look for things that are wrong with your child. Doctors help your sick child get well and heal broken bones. Doctors find ear infections and heart murmurs. And realistically, doctors have precious little time to spend hearing about your child's potty training struggles. I don't mean that as any sort of slight against doctors.

I think part of it is our health care system and the speed at which we need to be seen. I also think doctors tend to look at moms like we're whack-jobs. Let's face it: we can all be a little crazy in the doctor's office. Okay — I can, at least.

Here are some soundbites from appointments with Pascal's pediatrician:

"How's he eating?" She's looking for general answers, not the blow-by-blow I want to give her.

"How are his stools?" She's looking for solid vs. mushy, gray vs. brown, not the minutia I'd like to give her.

"He likes kindergarten?" She's looking for me to tell her that everything is normal, not every frigging cute thing he tells me everyday.

So, when the pediatrician asks if your child is potty training, she means it should be on your radar. She doesn't want to see a poop log. It's just not a pediatrician's area of expertise, nor do they want it to be. The average pediatrician hasn't actually potty trained a variety of kids. Don't get me wrong — if you think there's a medical reason for your child's potty training troubles, ASK!!! But don't expect solutions to non-medical problems. Bottom line: your pediatrician is busy with the job of keeping your child healthy and well. You can't expect them to know everything about everything.

Penises and potty training (or is it peni?)

The title says it all. I get a fair number of inquiries about the penis, as it relates to potty training.

Standing to pee: When do boys start to stand up to pee? The best time to start is when he's actually tall enough for his penis to clear the toilet bowl. When they're first potty trained, this isn't usually the case. You don't want to mess around with a step stool, a toddler and a big porcelain bowl. When you start with the potty, have him sit on the potty chair or toilet insert. These sometimes come with a pee guard that I've never heard, even once, of working. The best thing to do is just tell him, "Hold your penis down." You can gently put his legs together to help him do this. Most boys don't mind touching their penises, so it shouldn't be a problem. When you start like this, it quickly becomes habit.

When he is tall enough or old enough to reach the potty with his penis while standing, you can have him push up on the skin right above the penis, as opposed to holding the penis for aim. This gives him a great amount of control and eliminates the whole "loaded gun in his hands" issue. Yes, once boys figure out they can hold it and aim, it does quickly become a game, so if you can stop that from the get-go, you'll be better off. I know some people suggest cereal in the toilet to practice aiming, but again, I think this just sets up potential for a mess. Plus, it's pee. Do you really want to make a big game about it? It's your call.

One thing I hear a lot is: "But he wants to pee just like his dad." Absolutely no offense, but this is kind of lame. Dad does tons of things that his boy can't do yet. You can simply say, "When you get a little bit bigger, then you can pee like Daddy." Don't make it an issue, and your child won't either.

If you start off teaching him to lift the seat, be very careful if you have any sort of cover on the toilet lid. The cover adds padding, and the lid can sometimes slam shut. Good luck with potty training after he's slammed his penis in the toilet seat. Yikes.

Also, even at this young age, if there's dribble on the seat or bowl edge, teach him to wipe it off with some TP. Future generations of women will thank you.

Circumcised vs. uncircumcised: Is there a difference in potty training for circumcised versus uncircumcised penises? The answer is no. The process is exactly the same. I have noticed that with the foreskin intact, the penis hangs down a bit more, which makes aiming a bit easier at first. Also, there have been questions as to whether the foreskin could hold a mini-reservoir of pee. Again, no. If you've got a dribbler, it's the kid, not the penis.

Okay. That's all I've got on penises. If you've got a random penis question, feel free to ask. I'd prefer it relate to potty training, but hey, I'm open to any random penis question. I can't say I'm an expert but...you know...

Other questions and their answers

When can I move the potty chair to the bathroom?
This is a question I get asked a **lot**. It is totally your call.

Usually, it happens when you get sick of the potty chair being in the living room (or playroom or kitchen). A lot of this will depend on your house set-up. There will be an indefinable moment when you know your child can make it to the bathroom. There's usually just a natural progression toward your child wanting privacy and/or knowing the bathroom is **the** place for the potty. If you are unsure about whether or not she can actually make it, keep the potty chair where it's handy. Set her up for success — don't put barriers in her way.

When can I switch to the big toilet? Same goes for the switch to the big toilet and ditching the potty chair altogether. Over time, around a month or so after potty training, you should be regularly offering the big toilet over the little potty and your child should start getting used to both. Most kids gravitate towards the toilet, again with that sense that it is the right place to be. If your child really loves the potty, it's okay. Eventually, the infatuation fades. I've never, ever had a weird situation, like a 5-year-old who will only use the little potty. Go with your gut.

When can I get rid of the insert? Once again, same deal with the insert. It's just a matter of when your child is ready to let it go. Don't rush ditching the insert. Your child's bum isn't going to be big enough for the toilet seat for quite some time, and if she falls into the toilet, you can kiss all your hard work goodbye.

When will he start wiping his own butt? When you feel like you can deal with the crappy job he does of wiping his own butt. Kidding. No, I'm not. Once again, your call. My son just turned six and we split the duty. You both will come to some agreement at some point.

How should I sanitize the potty chair? Do not use hardcore sanitizers on the potty chair — a baby wipe will be fine. If you are using Clorox or something similar, your child may get a rash. This is particularly true of girls, whose yonis tend to rub against the potty chair.

What does "done" look like? How will I know my kid is potty trained? There's no defined marker for "done" when it comes to potty training. Most children may have an accident or two after being "done." You can't say — although I've heard it plenty — that once a kid is potty trained, there are no accidents. Our children are human. They can be unsure, scared, emotional, overjoyed — and any of these can bring on an accident. They can be teething, feverish, have an ear infection or be over-tired. Any can bring on an accident. For me, I think "done" is when potty training fades into the fabric of your life. You will have to prompt occasionally, you will have insist sometimes, you may have to change her clothes once in a while, but none of it will seem earth-shattering. For most moms, they mark "done" in their heads with potty success during increasingly challenging or exciting events. *Disney on Ice* — no accidents — whoo-hoo!! Went to grandma's for 3 days — no accidents — whoo hoo! Took a 5-hour car ride — peed at the rest stops — whoo hoo! Like any other skill, your child's ability to use the potty gets better and better until you're no longer thinking about it ALL. THE. TIME. On the flip side, if your child is having an accident every single day...that's not "done." Go back and tighten the process. Run through the blocks of learning real fast. Clean up the frayed edges a bit. And remember, don't let anyone else determine what "done" means to you and your family.

Chapter 20: Parting Words, Mama-a-Mama

If things start falling apart or it's not going as planned, try to PINPOINT what exactly is going on, and where it went wrong. Narrow it down. Most parents get overwhelmed and think, "My kid is just not potty training." That's rarely true. Usually there's some singular component that messing everything up. Try to find that singular component.

When I consult with parents, that's exactly what I do. I strip it all down and try to find and focus on the one thing that's really the root of the problem.

Break down the bad and break down the GOOD. Bounce between the blocks if you need to. Nothing is law, and nothing is written in stone. Play around with backing off and moving back in with prompting. Also, remember: there's no big finish line. This isn't a contest, nor is it a measure of your parenting ability.

That's all folks. That's everything I know about potty training, in broad sweeping strokes. I highly suggest you check out the blog and our Facebook page. I'm always learning new things and I keep my thoughts current in those places.

I'm available for one-on-one consulting, but I encourage you to find the answers here. Not because I don't want to help you, but because you don't need to lean on me. There's a dance and a rhythm to potty training just like everything else. FIND YOUR WAY. Take what I've said and craft it — make it yours and your child's. Many, many parents panic the first day. It's okay. Keep going. You might feel like a crappy teacher. Keep going. You might feel like your kid is being utterly ridiculous about this. Keep going. It's just another milestone — just another something you are teaching your child.

A parting thought: while I have given you the curriculum, YOU ARE THE EXPERT ON YOUR CHILD. You hold the magic keys. And I know you can do it. And I know your kid can do it. I have full faith and confidence in you.

Rock on, Mama!!!

Dads' Cheat Sheet:

(Once again, I mean no slight to Dads who are reading this and taking part in potty training. I know you're busy so here's a quick list)

Hey Dads. So listen. This potty training thing **has** to be done at some point. The earlier the better. Yes, I know you probably don't want to deal with it when you are tired and come home at the end of the day. And your partner might be a little insane for a few days.

It's all good. **This is temporary.** All of it. Your kid is going to be so proud of himself when he's done. You will be so proud when he's done. And you won't be spending any more money on diapers. Yay! So please, please, do right by your child and help with this as much as possible.

Here are the major points to remember:

Your kid is untrustworthy at this point. You cannot just ask him if he has to go. He'll say NO, cause it's his favorite word, and then you are screwed.

Don't **ask**, period. Never ask if he has to go. Tell and bring. If you see or know he's got to go — he's dancing around, looking uncomfortable — you say, "Come. Time to pee."

Use your own leverage as Dad. Your kid loves you in a really special way that is different than Mom. Use that power for good. Enjoy whatever special time you two have together, but make him **pee first**.

Video games, wrestling, TV watching...**pee first**. Say that. "You pee first and then we'll...."

Don't act helpless. You know your kid just as well as your partner, but in a different way.

Keep your eyes open looking for your kid's pee pee dance.

Don't hover, and don't prompt him every two seconds. Can you imagine anything worse than someone on you like white on rice, asking you to pee when you don't have to?

Be casual and cool. You probably already have that role anyway. You can be casual and nonchalant and good cop and still watch out for pee.

Your partner is going to go cuckoo. I promise she'll return to normal very soon. Get her drunk. It's okay.

Do your best to help, even if you don't want to. This has to get done. Might as well be now.

Your role in this is **just as vital** as Mom's is. Maybe more. Everyone knows that Dad is a little magic.

19515828R00167

Made in the USA
San Bernardino, CA
01 March 2015